The Chicken Cookbook

FEATURING
RECIPES
FROM
THE
42nd
NATIONAL
CHICKEN
COOKING
CONTEST ®

THE CHICKEN COOKBOOK
A Bantam Premium Book/April 1997

Cover Photograph: Spicy Grilled Chicken Thighs with Salsa
(recipe on page 104)

Contents

All the World Loves Chicken

Chicken is not only America's, but also one of the world's favorite meats. There's hardly a culture or religion that does not include chicken in its diet.

Consumption of chicken in the United States increased dramatically in the past quarter century, doubling from about 37 pounds per capita in 1970 to about 74 pounds today. By the year 2000, chicken consumption is expected to exceed 80 pounds per person annually.

Today's chicken is a convenience food, packaged in numerous time-saving ways. Gone are the days when a whole bird was the consumer's only choice. Fresh chicken is now available in an array of cut-up parts, boned, skinned, diced, ground, marinated — all making it easier to prepare tempting, wholesome dishes for family meals or entertaining.

Chicken provides the complete protein which the body needs daily. It is low in fat content and in calories. Its delicate flavor adapts well to most other foods and seasonings. It is the choice meat of chefs for creative dishes. Yet it can easily be prepared by the novice cook.

It's no wonder that chicken is enjoyed by so many so often. Chicken is tasty, nutritious, economical and so versatile it can be prepared in literally hundreds of different ways, as recipes in this book attest. Try them and discover why chicken's popularity continues to soar, both in America and around the globe.

Cook-Off Finalists

The 51 finalists in the
National Chicken Cooking
Contest are each already
winners, chosen from
thousands of entries as the
best recipe from every state
and the District of Columbia.
These are the recipes
prepared at the 42nd National
Cook-Off in Hilton Head,
South Carolina. From them
judges had the difficult task
of selecting the $25,000 first
prize winner and the four
others to share an additional
$11,000 in prize money.

Yucatan-Thai Chicken Fajitas

4 boneless, skinless chicken breast halves, cut in strips	1 can (4 oz.) chopped green chilies
1 teaspoon seasoned salt	2 tablespoons chopped fresh mint
2 tablespoons vegetable oil	8 flour tortillas (7-inch)
½ cup thinly sliced red bell pepper	Apricot-Hoisin Sauce: recipe follows
3 cups broccoli slaw mix	¼ cup toasted sunflower seed
2 green onions, cut in 1-inch pieces	mint sprigs

Sprinkle chicken with seasoned salt. In large frypan, place vegetable oil over medium-high heat. Add chicken and cook, stirring, about 4 minutes or until tender. Add red pepper, broccoli slaw, green onions, chilies and mint; cook about 4 minutes longer, stirring. Warm tortillas according to package directions. Spread each tortilla with Apricot-Hoisin Sauce. Divide chicken mixture equally among tortillas, sprinkle with sunflower kernels, fold up and arrange on serving platter. Garnish with mint sprigs. Makes 4 servings.

Apricot-Hoisin Sauce: In small bowl, mix together ⅓ cup hoisin sauce, ⅓ cup apricot preserves, 2 tablespoons peanut butter, ½ teaspoon dark sesame oil, 1 teaspoon minced garlic and ⅛ teaspoon pepper.

Maggie Little, Huntsville, AL

Chicken Condiment Curry

4	boneless, skinless chicken breast halves	3	cans (10¾ oz.) golden mushroom soup
¼	teaspoon onion powder	2	teaspoons mild curry powder
¼	teaspoon tarragon		
3	tablespoons butter	1	cup peeled, diced tart apples
¾	cup coarsely chopped onion	4	cups cooked rice
¾	cup chopped green pepper		Condiments to pass: suggestions follow
¾	cup thinly sliced celery		

In medium saucepan, place chicken breasts and enough water to cover. Add onion powder and tarragon. Place over high heat and bring to a boil. Reduce heat and simmer about 15 minutes or until fork can be inserted in chicken with ease. Remove chicken from pan and cool, reserving ¾ cup of the liquid. Cut chicken into ½-inch cubes. In large saucepan over medium heat, melt butter. Add onion, green pepper and celery; sauté about 5 minutes or until tender. Add mushroom soup, reserved liquid, chicken, curry powder and apples, stirring gently. Bring to a boil, reduce heat and simmer, covered, about 10 minutes or until apples are tender. Makes 4 servings.

Condiments: Suggested assortment to serve as topping; chutney, sliced green onions, chopped peanuts, shredded coconut, crumbled bacon, chopped hard cooked eggs, chopped green pepper, raisins.

Roberta Ford, Anchorage, AK

Tuscan Walnut Chicken

4 boneless, skinless chicken breast halves
½ cup crumbled Gorgonzola cheese
2 egg whites, slightly beaten
2 tablespoons plain nonfat yogurt
2 teaspoons lemon juice
¾ cup ground walnuts
1 teaspoon nutmeg
½ teaspoon salt
   Fresh Pear Walnut Glaze: recipe follows
   pear slices
   walnut halves
2 tablespoons minced Italian parsley

With sharp knife, cut chicken breasts horizontally ¾ way through meat. Open breasts, place between 2 sheets of plastic wrap and gently pound to uniform thickness. Divide cheese equally on half of each chicken breast; fold over opposite half and press edges together to seal. In shallow bowl, mix together egg whites, yogurt and lemon juice. In another shallow dish, mix together ground walnuts, nutmeg and salt. Dip chicken, one piece at a time, first in egg mixture and then in walnut mixture, turning to coat. Arrange chicken in shallow baking dish sprayed with nonstick vegetable spray; refrigerate 20 minutes. Place chicken in 350°F. oven and bake about 20 minutes or until fork can be inserted with ease. Place chicken breasts on individual serving plates and spoon on Fresh Pear Walnut Glaze. Garnish with pear slices and walnut halves; sprinkle with parsley. Makes 4 servings.

Fresh Pear Walnut Glaze: In frypan over medium heat, place 1 tablespoon vegetable oil. Add ¼ cup minced onion and 1 teaspoon grated lemon rind; sauté 2 minutes. Stir in 1 cup pear juice and ¼ cup white wine; simmer 5 minutes. Add 2 teaspoons Dijon mustard, stirring and cooking about 2 minutes until slightly thickened. Add 1 cored and thinly sliced pear and ¼ cup toasted walnut halves.

Judith Perkins, Scottsdale, AZ

Pharaonic Chicken

4 boneless, skinless chicken breast halves

4 boneless, skinless chicken thighs

½ teaspoon allspice

2½ teaspoons salt, divided

½ teaspoon cumin

⅓ teaspoon cinnamon

1 tablespoon sugar

⅓ cup olive oil

1½ pounds baking potatoes, peeled and cut in ½-inch circles

4 cloves garlic, minced

½ cup fresh lemon juice

4 tablespoons grated Romano cheese

In medium bowl, place allspice, 1½ teaspoons of the salt, cumin, cinnamon, sugar and olive oil; stir to mix well. Add chicken and marinate 15 minutes. Boil potatoes in water to cover and remaining 1 teaspoon salt, about 10 minutes or until tender but not soft; drain. In large baking pan, place chicken in single layer and bake in 425°F. oven for 20 minutes. Remove chicken from oven and arrange potato rings between pieces. In small dish, mix together garlic and lemon juice; pour over chicken and potatoes. Return to oven and bake an additional 12 minutes. Sprinkle with cheese and return to oven until cheese melts. Makes 6 servings.

Emad Saleh, Fayetteville, AR

Yucatan Chicken with Peach-Avocado Salsa

6	boneless, skinless chicken breast halves
1	tablespoon, plus 1 teaspoon garlic pepper seasoning
1	orange, juiced
1	lime, juiced
2	tablespoons olive oil
1	teaspoon dried oregano leaves
	Peach-Avocado Salsa: recipe follows
	lime slices

Place chicken in shallow glass dish; rub all sides with garlic pepper seasoning. Pour orange and lime juices over chicken; drizzle with olive oil. Crush oregano with fingers and sprinkle over chicken. Cover and refrigerate 30 minutes, turning once. Remove chicken from marinade and place in large nonstick frypan over medium heat. Sauté, turning, about 12 minutes or until lightly browned and fork can be inserted in chicken with ease. Serve topped with Peach-Avocado Salsa; garnish with lime slices.

Peach-Avocado Salsa: In medium bowl, mix together 1 fresh peach, peeled, pitted and diced; 1 small avocado, peeled, pitted and diced; 1 tomato, peeled, seeded and diced; ¼ cup diced jicama; 3 tablespoons chopped red onion and 2 tablespoons chopped fresh cilantro. In small bowl, whisk together ¼ teaspoon crushed red pepper flakes, 3 tablespoons fresh lime juice and 2 teaspoons olive oil; pour into peach-avocado mixture, stirring gently.

Teresa Hannan Smith, Santa Rosa, CA

Roasted Balsamic Chicken with Sautéed Vegetables

1	whole broiler-fryer chicken	1	teaspoon freshly ground pepper
¼	cup balsamic vinegar	1	teaspoon salt
¼	cup extra virgin olive oil	1	teaspoon dried sage
1	tablespoon brown sugar		Sautéed Vegetables: recipe follows

In small bowl, mix together vinegar, olive oil, sugar, pepper, salt and sage. Place 2 tablespoons mixture in cavity of chicken; rotate to coat thoroughly. Hook wing tips under back of chicken and place chicken, breast side up, in shallow baking pan. Spoon remaining vinegar mixture over chicken, rubbing into top and sides. Place in 350°F. oven for about 1 hour, basting with pan juices after 30 minutes. Chicken is done when internal temperature of 180°F. is reached or when fork can be inserted with ease and legs and wings move easily. Let rest 10 minutes; reserve pan juices. Place chicken on platter with sautéed vegetables around edges; spoon some of reserved pan juices over all. Makes 4 servings.

Sautéed Vegetables: In large nonstick frypan, place 2 tablespoons extra virgin olive oil over medium-high heat. Add ½ cup chopped yellow onion and sauté 1 minute. Add 1 red bell pepper, sliced into rings; ½ cup diagonally sliced celery and 1 clove garlic, finely minced; stir-fry 2 more minutes. Add 1 cup sliced mushrooms; cook 2 minutes; stir in 1 tablespoon balsamic vinegar, ½ teaspoon freshly ground pepper and ½ teaspoon salt.

Sandra Collins, Wheat Ridge, CO

Pan-Seared Chicken Scapece

6	boneless, skinless chicken breast halves	3	tablespoons balsamic vinegar
½	cup golden raisins	¼	cup low-sodium chicken broth
½	cup white wine	6	medium cloves garlic, coarsely chopped, divided
1	lemon, halved		
1	tablespoon coarsely ground pepper	2	small red chiles, seeded, chopped, divided
1	teaspoon ground coriander		
½	teaspoon kosher salt	2	tablespoons fresh tarragon
2	tablespoons extra virgin olive oil, divided		

In small dish, place raisins; add wine and let soak. Rub lemon over chicken, squeezing to release juice. In small dish, mix together pepper, coriander and salt; rub onto chicken. In large nonstick frypan over high heat, place 1 tablespoon of the olive oil. Add chicken and sear on both sides; remove from pan and keep warm. To frypan, add vinegar, chicken broth, ½ of the chopped garlic, ½ of the chiles and raisins with wine. Boil 1 minute, return chicken to pan, lower heat, cover and continue to cook about 12 minutes more, or until fork can be inserted in chicken with ease. Remove chicken to serving dish. To frypan, add remaining 1 tablespoon of the olive oil, remaining garlic and remaining chiles; pour over chicken. Garnish with tarragon. Makes 6 servings.

Susan Miller, Wilton, CT

Italian Style Chicken Wings

2½ pounds chicken wings

2 tablespoons olive oil

3 cloves garlic, crushed

¼ teaspoon oregano

1 teaspoon parsley flakes

¼ cup grated Parmigiano cheese

½ teaspoon salt

¼ teaspoon pepper

¼ cup balsamic vinegar

radicchio leaves

curly parsley

Cut wings at each joint; discard tips. Place joints in shallow baking pan; sprinkle with olive oil, garlic, oregano, parsley flakes, Parmigiano cheese, salt and pepper. Place in 350°F. oven for about 45 minutes. Remove from oven, pour vinegar over chicken and place under broiler about 4 minutes on each side. Garnish serving platter with radicchio and parsley. Makes about 24 drummettes.

Diana Carr, Hockessin, DE

Sublime Sub-Continental Chicken Curry

4	boneless, skinless chicken breasts	1	large cucumber, peeled, seeded, thinly sliced
2	tablespoons canola oil	2	tablespoons chopped mint leaves
3	large onions, quartered, sliced	2	teaspoons seasoned salt
3	large garlic cloves, sliced	4	cups water
3	tablespoons mild curry paste	2	cups basmati rice
3	tablespoons ginger pickle	1	tablespoon turmeric
		$\frac{1}{2}$	teaspoon salt
3	boxes (10 oz.) frozen chopped spinach, thawed	1	box (10 oz.) frozen peas, thawed
3	cups chicken broth	5	drops red food color
3	cups nonfat yogurt	8	papadums

Cut chicken into bite-size chunks; set aside. In large frypan over medium heat, place oil. Add onions and garlic and sauté about 7 minutes. Stir in curry paste and ginger pickle; cook 5 minutes more. Add spinach, chicken and broth; cook, uncovered, about 20 minutes or until fork can be inserted in chicken with ease. In large bowl, mix together yogurt, cucumber, mint and seasoned salt; set aside. In large saucepan, place water and bring to a boil. Add rice, salt and turmeric; cover and cook until fluffy, about 15 minutes. Add peas and food color; let sit 7 minutes, then toss carefully to mix. In oven set on broil, place papadums on middle rack, leaving door open; heat about 30 seconds, turn and cook 15 seconds more, taking care not to burn. On large platter, place rice with chicken mixture in center. Pass yogurt-cucumber mixture and papadums. Makes 8 servings.

Annie Groer, Washington, DC

Chicken with Portobello Sunflower Sauce

4	boneless, skinless chicken breast halves, cut in bite-size pieces	1	shallot, minced
1/2	teaspoon salt	1	garlic clove, minced
1/4	teaspoon pepper	1/2	cup chicken broth
3	teaspoons margarine, divided	2	tablespoons dry red wine
3	stemmed portobello mushrooms (3-inch), finely chopped	1/2	cup reduced-fat sour cream
3	tablespoons finely chopped dry roasted sunflower nuts	1/2	tablespoon chopped fresh thyme
		4	cups hot cooked rice
		4	sprigs thyme

Sprinkle chicken with salt and pepper. In large nonstick frypan, place 1½ teaspoons of the margarine over medium heat. Add chicken and stir-fry about 5 minutes or until fork can be inserted with ease. Remove chicken from frypan and cover with foil to keep warm. Add remaining 1½ teaspoons margarine to frypan. Stir in mushrooms, sunflower nuts, shallot and garlic; sauté about 3 minutes. Add chicken broth and red wine and cook about 2 minutes more to reduce liquid slightly. Lower heat to medium-low and stir in sour cream and thyme. Return chicken to frypan to heat through. Place rice on serving platter and top with chicken and sauce. Garnish with sprigs of fresh thyme. Makes 4 servings.

Eileen Watson, Oviedo, FL

Baked Greek Chicken Salad

4	boneless, skinless chicken breast halves	1	package mixed Italian salad greens
¼	cup melted butter		Tomato-Cucumber Salsa: recipe follows
1	lemon, juiced		
¼	teaspoon freshly ground pepper	2	ounces feta cheese, crumbled
½	teaspoon garlic powder		black olives
1	teaspoon oregano		pepperoncini pepper
1	teaspoon Greek seasoning		

Place chicken in baking dish. In medium bowl, mix together butter, lemon juice, pepper, garlic powder, oregano and Greek seasoning; pour over chicken. Place chicken in 350°F. oven and bake for about 50 minutes, uncovered, basting occasionally. Place salad greens in large serving bowl. Top with Tomato-Cucumber Salsa. Slice chicken in thin strips and arrange on top of salad. Sprinkle with feta cheese and garnish with olives and pepper. Makes 4 servings.

Tomato-Cucumber Salsa: In medium bowl, mix together 2 diced plum tomatoes, 1 peeled and sliced small cucumber, ½ green pepper julienned, ¼ sliced purple onion, 2 tablespoons red wine vinegar, 1 tablespoon olive oil, 2 tablespoons vegetable oil and ⅛ teaspoon *each* freshly ground pepper, salt, basil, oregano, Greek seasoning, sugar and dry mustard. Chill until ready to serve.

Pamela Mazaris, Macon, GA

Rosemary-Garlic Roasted Chicken

1	whole broiler-fryer chicken	1	teaspoon freshly ground pepper
2	teaspoons rock salt	2	tablespoons olive oil
4	cloves garlic, minced	1	tablespoon white wine
2	tablespoons minced rosemary		rosemary sprigs

Loosen skin by placing fingers between skin and meat, beginning at neck and gently working way around breast to drumsticks. In small bowl, mix together salt, garlic, minced rosemary, pepper, olive oil and wine; rub mixture under skin and in cavity of chicken. Place rosemary sprigs in cavity, tie legs together and place on roasting rack coated with cooking spray. Place in 325°F. oven and cook about 1 hour 45 minutes or until fork can be inserted in chicken with ease. Garnish with fresh rosemary sprigs. Makes 4 servings.

Judith Matoba, Mililani, HI

Moroccan Chicken Kabobs

1¼ pounds boneless, skinless chicken thighs, cut in 2-inch pieces

1 tablespoon lemon juice

1 tablespoon minced fresh ginger

1½ teaspoons cumin

1 teaspoon sesame oil

1 teaspoon ground coriander

½ teaspoon paprika

¼ teaspoon cinnamon

2 medium zucchini, cut in 1½-inch pieces

8 cherry tomatoes

1 tablespoon vegetable oil

¾ teaspoon salt

½ teaspoon freshly ground pepper

1½ cups chicken broth

1 tablespoon butter

1 cup couscous

½ cup chopped green onion

In medium bowl, mix together lemon juice, ginger, cumin, sesame oil, coriander, paprika and cinnamon. Add chicken, cover and refrigerate at least 30 minutes. Loosely thread 4 skewers,* alternating chicken with vegetables. Brush lightly with vegetable oil; sprinkle with salt and pepper. Arrange on broiler pan sprayed with nonstick cooking spray and place in oven. Broil about 4 inches from heat, turning occasionally, about 12 minutes or until fork can be inserted in chicken with ease. In medium saucepan over high heat, place chicken broth and butter and bring to a boil; stir in couscous. Remove from heat, cover and let stand 5 minutes. Stir in green onions. Arrange couscous on platter with kabobs on top. Makes 4 servings.

Suzan Ward, Coeur d'Alene, ID

* If using wooden skewers, soak in warm water for 30 minutes to prevent burning.

Chicken Gorgonzola Roulades

4	boneless, skinless chicken breast halves	2	tablespoons pine nuts
¼	teaspoon salt	1	tablespoon olive oil
⅛	teaspoon pepper		Spicy Red Pepper Sauce: recipe follows
16	large basil leaves		basil leaves
½	cup crumbled Gorgonzola cheese		

Gently pound chicken breasts to ¼-inch thickness; sprinkle with salt and pepper. Place 4 basil leaves over each piece of chicken, covering entirely. Sprinkle 2 tablespoons of cheese over basil. In large frypan over medium-high heat, toast pine nuts, shaking pan occasionally, until lightly browned, about 3 minutes. Sprinkle ½ tablespoon of the pine nuts over each chicken breast half. Tightly roll breasts, starting with short end; secure with wooden picks. To same frypan, add olive oil. Add chicken and sauté, turning frequently, about 10 minutes or until brown on all sides. Reduce heat to low, cover and simmer an additional 10 minutes, or until fork can be inserted in chicken with ease. Remove chicken to cutting board and let rest about 10 minutes. Spoon Spicy Red Pepper Sauce evenly on 4 individual serving plates. Slice each chicken roll into ½-inch slices and arrange, overlapping slices slightly, on top of sauce. Garnish with basil leaves. Makes 4 servings.

Spicy Red Pepper Sauce: In blender container, place 1 jar (12 oz.) roasted red peppers (drained), ½ cup tomato puree, 2 cloves garlic, 1 teaspoon sugar, ½ teaspoon salt and ¼ teaspoon red pepper flakes. Pour into medium saucepan and heat over medium-low heat.

Debbie Vanni, Libertyville, IL

Thai Chicken with Mango Slaw

6   boneless, skinless chicken breast halves

2   tablespoons honey

2   tablespoons vegetable oil

3   tablespoons lime juice

1/2 teaspoon salt

1/4 teaspoon pepper

3   cups shredded red cabbage

2   cups shredded savoy

1   cup peeled, julienned carrots

1   ripe mango, peeled, seeded, cut in 1/2-inch pieces

Peanut Sauce: recipe follows

3   tablespoons chopped scallions

3   tablespoons chopped peanuts

Flatten chicken breast halves slightly with palm of hand. Spray broiler pan with nonstick vegetable spray, arrange chicken on pan and place in oven set on BROIL about 4 inches from heat source. Broil about 7 minutes, turn and continue cooking about 6 minutes more or until fork can be inserted in chicken with ease. In small bowl, mix together honey, vegetable oil, lime juice, salt and pepper. In large bowl, place red cabbage, savoy and carrots; toss to mix well. Add honey-lime mixture and mango, tossing gently. Arrange cabbage mixture on platter with chicken on top. Spoon Peanut Sauce over chicken and sprinkle with scallions and peanuts. Makes 6 servings.

Peanut Sauce: In small bowl, whisk together 4 tablespoons creamy peanut butter, 2 tablespoons water, 2 tablespoons honey, 4 tablespoons lime juice, 2 tablespoons soy sauce and 1/2 teaspoon hot red pepper flakes.

Tara Meier, Greenwood, IN

Plum Chicken

4   boneless, skinless
    chicken breast halves

1   medium onion,
    chopped

½   cup bottled Italian
    dressing

⅓   cup soy sauce

2   tablespoons molasses

2   plums, pitted, sliced

Arrange chicken in baking dish. Sprinkle onion over and around chicken. In small bowl, mix together dressing, soy sauce and molasses; pour over chicken. Place plum slices on top of breast halves. Place chicken in 425°F. oven and bake for about 35 minutes or until fork can be inserted in chicken with ease. Makes 4 servings.

Katherine Shipley, Cedar Rapids, IA

Roasted Nut Chicken Pate

4	boneless, skinless chicken breast halves	4	green onions
½	cup water	1	teaspoon thyme
¼	cup cream sherry	1	teaspoon basil
1	cup broken walnuts	¼	teaspoon salt
1	cup slivered almonds	½	teaspoon freshly ground pepper
¾	cup cream	⅛	teaspoon red pepper
4	tablespoons sherry		fresh basil leaves
4	tablespoons mayonnaise	½	sweet red pepper, finely diced

In medium frypan with lid, place chicken, water and cream sherry. Place over medium heat and poach about 20 minutes; drain and set aside to cool. On cookie sheet, place walnuts and almonds in 400°F. oven for about 10 minutes, stirring once. In food processor, place cream, sherry, mayonnaise, green onions, thyme, basil, salt, pepper and red pepper; mix. Add chicken and all but 2 tablespoons roasted nuts; process to form creamy mixture. Press in bowl. Garnish with the reserved 2 tablespoons roasted nuts, fresh basil and diced red pepper. Marinate in refrigerator up to 2 days or serve immediately with crackers, toasted pitas and/or bagel slices.

Toni Terrell, Shawnee Mission, KS

Szechuan Chicken Pasta Salad

4	boneless, skinless chicken breast halves, cut in thin strips	½	cup chopped green onions
3	tablespoons light soy sauce	½	cup finely grated carrot
¼	teaspoon sugar	½	cup seeded and grated cucumber
¼	teaspoon crushed red pepper flakes	1½	cups fresh bean sprouts, rinsed and drained
2	tablespoons sesame oil		Dressing: recipe follows
½	pound vermicelli, cooked according to package directions	1	tablespoon sesame seeds

In glass bowl, mix together soy sauce, sugar and red pepper flakes. Add chicken strips, turning to coat; cover and marinate in refrigerator 20 minutes. In frypan, place sesame oil over high heat. Add chicken strips and stir-fry about 5 minutes or until chicken is lightly browned. Remove chicken from frypan and cool. In large bowl, place vermicelli, chicken, green onions, carrots, cucumber and bean sprouts; toss gently to mix well. Pour dressing over mixture and stir until well coated. Refrigerate 30 minutes, arrange on platter and sprinkle with sesame seeds. Makes 4 servings.

Dressing: In small bowl, whisk together ½ cup water, 6 tablespoons light soy sauce, 3 tablespoons peanut butter, 2 tablespoons cider vinegar, 2 teaspoons sugar and ⅛ teaspoon crushed red pepper flakes.

Laura Albrecht, California, KY

Apple Chicken Delight

4   boneless, skinless
     chicken breast halves
¼ cup flour
½ teaspoon cinnamon
½ teaspoon salt
3   tablespoons canola oil
½ cup apple cider

1   tablespoon cornstarch
½ cup pineapple
     preserves
¼ cup toasted pecans,
     coarsely chopped
spiced apple rings
pecan halves

In shallow dish, place flour. Sprinkle chicken with cinnamon and
salt. Dredge chicken in flour, one piece at a time. In large
frypan, place canola oil over medium heat. Add chicken and
cook, turning frequently, about 20 minutes or until light brown
and fork can be inserted with ease. Remove chicken to serving
platter and keep warm. Pour off liquid from frypan and add
apple cider. Slowly whisk in cornstarch, mixing well. Stir in
pineapple preserves. Add pecans and simmer until thickened,
about 3 minutes. Pour sauce over chicken and garnish with
apple rings and pecan halves. Makes 4 servings.

Alma Hemelt, Chalmette, LA

Tropical Chicken

4   boneless, skinless
    chicken breast halves

1   tablespoon extra virgin
    olive oil

2   tablespoons unsalted
    butter

1   large egg, slightly
    beaten

1   teaspoon water

1   teaspoon salt

½   teaspoon pepper

1   cup, firmly packed,
    flaked coconut

1   teaspoon cornstarch

¼   cup orange juice

½   cup sweet orange
    marmalade

    peeled and sliced kiwi

    parsley sprigs

Place chicken between 2 pieces of wax paper and gently pound
to ¼-inch thickness. In small bowl, place egg, water, salt and
pepper; stir to mix well. In shallow dish, place coconut. Dredge
chicken, first in egg mixture, then in coconut, pressing to coat
well. In large nonstick frypan, place olive oil and butter over
medium heat. Add chicken and cook, turning once, about 10
minutes or until brown and fork can be inserted with ease.
Remove chicken to serving platter and keep warm. In small
dish, place cornstarch. Add orange juice and stir to mix well. In
small saucepan, place marmalade. Stir in orange juice mixture
and cook over low heat, stirring, to thicken but do not boil.
Spoon orange sauce over chicken. Garnish with kiwi slices and
parsley sprigs. Makes 4 servings.

Thomas Goodman, Harrison, ME

Chicken with Roasted Peppers and Dilled Marsala Cream

4	boneless, skinless chicken breast halves	½	cup plus 2 tablespoons grated Parmesan cheese, divided
3	tablespoons flour	4	ounces lowfat cream cheese, cubed
½	teaspoon freshly ground pepper	1	tablespoon plus 1 teaspoon lemon juice
½	teaspoon garlic powder	3	tablespoons finely chopped dill
¼	teaspoon salt		
3	teaspoons olive oil, divided	4	cups hot, cooked linguine
1½	cups low sodium chicken broth	2	tablespoons lightly toasted pine nuts
½	package (1.8 oz.) leek soup mix	1	starfruit, sliced and seeded
⅓	cup Marsala wine		dill sprigs
4	ounces shiitake mushrooms, sliced		
1	jar (7 oz.) roasted red peppers, drained, cut into 1-inch strips		

Cut each chicken breast half almost in half horizontally, taking care not to separate. Open each half, place between sheets of plastic wrap and gently flatten to uniform thickness. In shallow plate, mix together flour, pepper, garlic powder and salt; dredge chicken in mixture to coat evenly. In large nonstick frypan over medium-high heat, place 2 teaspoons of the olive oil. Place half of chicken in pan and cook about 3 minutes on each side to brown; remove from heat and keep warm. Repeat with remaining oil and chicken. To frypan, add chicken broth. Gently whisk in leek soup mix, blending completely. Add Marsala wine and mushrooms; cook about 5 minutes, stirring occasionally. Stir in roasted peppers, ½ cup of the Parmesan cheese and cream cheese. When sauce is smooth, remove from heat and stir in lemon juice and dill. On large serving platter, arrange linguine. Spoon about two-thirds of sauce over the pasta; top with chicken. Drizzle remaining sauce over chicken, sprinkle with pine nuts and remaining 2 tablespoons Parmesan cheese. Garnish with dill sprigs and starfruit. Makes 4 servings.

Julia Fox, Annapolis, MD

Chicken Breasts with Portobello Mushrooms

2	whole boneless, skinless chicken breasts, halved	4	portobello mushrooms, sliced
¼	cup seasoned bread crumbs	1	tablespoon chopped parsley
¼	cup grated Parmesan cheese	¼	teaspoon pepper
1	small shallot, chopped	4	thin slices mozzarella cheese
1	tablespoon olive oil		

In shallow dish or on wax paper, mix together bread crumbs and Parmesan cheese. Press mixture into both sides of chicken. In small frypan, place olive oil over medium-high heat. Add shallot and sauté until soft. Add mushrooms, parsley and pepper; cook about 5 minutes, turning mushrooms once. Spray oven-proof casserole with nonstick cooking spray and arrange chicken flat in dish. Top with mushroom mixture, evenly divided over each piece. Arrange slice of mozzarella cheese on top. Place in 425°F. oven for 20 minutes or until fork can be inserted in chicken with ease. Makes 4 servings.

Maria Arsenault, Harwich, MA

Pumpkin Walnut Stuffed Chicken Breasts

4 chicken breast halves, boneless, with skin

½ cup canned pumpkin

¼ cup Italian seasoned bread crumbs

¼ cup raisins

¾ cup coarsely chopped walnuts, divided

½ teaspoon salt

¼ teaspoon pepper

⅔ cup apple butter

⅔ cup fat-free bottled Italian dressing

Gently pound chicken breasts to even thickness. In small bowl, mix together pumpkin, bread crumbs, raisins, ¼ cup of the walnuts, salt and pepper. With skin side of chicken down, place ¼ of the mixture in center of each breast half. Wrap chicken around mixture and fasten with wooden pick. Arrange chicken in shallow baking pan, seam side down, skin up. In small dish, mix together apple butter and Italian dressing; pour over chicken. Place in 350°F. oven and bake about 50 minutes, basting frequently with pan juices, until fork can be inserted in chicken with ease. Garnish with remaining ½ cup walnuts. Makes 4 servings.

Linda Kay Drysdale, Riverview, MI

Northern Exposure Chicken Burgers

1	pound ground chicken breast		Apple Yogurt Sauce: recipe follows
½	cup cooked wild or brown rice	4	sandwich buns
½	teaspoon nutmeg	4	teaspoons margarine
½	teaspoon salt		parsley sprigs
¼	teaspoon pepper		apple slices dipped in lemon juice

In medium bowl, mix together chicken, cooked rice, nutmeg, salt and pepper. Divide into 4 patties. Place on broiler pan and broil, about 4 inches from heat, about 5 minutes per side. Spread margarine lightly on inside of buns and toast in oven. Place chicken on toasted buns and spoon on Apple Yogurt Sauce. Garnish with parsley sprigs and apple slices. Makes 4 servings.

Apple Yogurt Sauce: In small bowl, mix together ½ cup plain yogurt, ¼ cup chopped unpeeled apple, 2 tablespoons chopped toasted pecans, 1 tablespoon chopped parsley and ½ teaspoon apple pie seasoning.

Gloria Kirchman, Eden Prairie, MN

Hawaiian Chicken

4 boneless, skinless chicken breast halves

¼ cup soy sauce

⅓ cup dry sherry

1 cup unsweetened pineapple juice

2 tablespoons red wine vinegar

3 tablespoons sugar

1 clove garlic, minced

1 cup crushed macadamia nuts

1 can (15¼ oz.) tropical fruit salad (reserve juice)

Tropical Sauce: recipe follows

In large resealable plastic bag, mix together soy sauce, sherry, pineapple juice, vinegar, sugar and garlic. Flatten chicken breasts to ¼-inch thickness, place in pineapple mixture and marinate in refrigerator for 20 minutes. Remove chicken and discard marinade. Roll chicken in crushed macadamia nuts and place in baking pan lightly sprayed with nonstick cooking spray. Bake in 350°F. oven for about 20 minutes or until fork can be inserted in chicken with ease. Pour tropical fruit salad over chicken and top with Tropical Sauce. Makes 4 servings.

Tropical Sauce: With small amount of juice from tropical fruit salad, mix 1 tablespoon cornstarch and stir until smooth. Add remaining fruit salad juice; stir in 1 tablespoon dry sherry and ½ teaspoon grated gingerroot. Place in small saucepan over low heat and cook about 2 minutes, stirring. Remove from heat and add 1 teaspoon grated lemon rind.

Regina Albright, Southaven, MS

Peppered Chicken and Cilantro Sandwiches

4 boneless, skinless chicken breast halves, cut in strips	1 large green bell pepper, julienned
6 tablespoons nonfat plain yogurt	1 large sweet red pepper, julienned
4 teaspoons Dijon mustard	1 medium white onion, thinly sliced
2 tablespoons grated Romano cheese	6 large sandwich buns, sliced and toasted inside
½ cup finely chopped cilantro leaves	6 large Romaine lettuce leaves
4 tablespoons olive oil	6 slices lowfat Swiss cheese

In small bowl, mix together yogurt, mustard, Romano cheese and cilantro; set aside. In large frypan, place olive oil over medium-high heat. Add chicken, green and red peppers and onion; stir-fry about 8 minutes or until fork can be inserted in chicken with ease. Brush each side of buns liberally with yogurt-cilantro mixture. Place 1 Romaine leaf on bottom part of each bun; top with slice of Swiss cheese. Add generous amount of chicken mixture and top of bun. Serve hot or wrap in plastic wrap and chill in refrigerator to serve cold. Makes 6 servings.

Patricia Neaves, Kansas City, MO

Chipotle Chicken Cassoulet

4 boneless, skinless chicken breast halves, cubed

2 tablespoons cooking oil

1 large onion, finely chopped

2 tablespoons minced garlic

1 teaspoon mustard seeds

1/4 teaspoon anise seed

2 cans (15 oz.) great Northern beans

10 canned chipotle peppers in adobo sauce, ground

1/2 cup dark molasses

1/4 cup orange juice concentrate

3 medium tomatoes, coarsely chopped

3 tablespoons butter

10 taco shells, finely crushed

1/2 cup grated Parmesan cheese

4 teaspoons sour cream

6 jalapeno peppers, halved and seeded

1/4 teaspoon paprika

In large frypan or Dutch oven, place oil over medium heat. Add onion, garlic, mustard seeds and anise seed; cook, stirring, about 2 minutes or until onion is translucent. Add chicken and cook, turning, about 10 minutes or until chicken has started to brown. Add beans, chipotle peppers, molasses, orange juice concentrate and tomatoes; continue cooking about 10 minutes until mixture is slightly thickened. In small frypan, place butter over medium heat. Add crushed taco shells and sauté until brown. Stir in Parmesan cheese and continue to cook, stirring, about 5 minutes more. Divide chicken mixture evenly in individual serving bowls and top with taco crumbs. Place 1 teaspoon sour cream in center of each and arrange peppers in pinwheel around sour cream. Sprinkle with paprika. Makes 4 servings.

Michael Mason, Joliet, MT

Spiced-Up Chicken Salad

4 boneless, skinless chicken breast halves

⅓ cup fresh lime juice

¼ cup olive oil

1 tablespoon soy sauce

2 tablespoons brown sugar

1 tablespoon finely minced basil

1 tablespoon finely minced mint

3 cloves garlic, divided

½ medium jalapeno pepper, minced

1 teaspoon finely grated ginger

½ teaspoon paprika

½ teaspoon freshly ground white pepper

1 large sweet red pepper, julienned

1 large sweet yellow pepper, julienned

1 small cucumber, quartered

2 cups torn lettuce leaves

2 cups torn spinach leaves

2 cups torn red lettuce leaves

Cut chicken into thin strips. In small bowl, mix together lime juice, olive oil, soy sauce, brown sugar, basil, mint and 1 clove of the garlic, minced; set aside. In nonstick frypan sprayed with cooking spray, place jalapeno pepper, remaining 2 cloves garlic and ginger; sauté 1 minute. Add chicken and stir-fry about 5 minutes or until fork can be inserted in chicken with ease. Remove chicken to large bowl and sprinkle with paprika and white pepper. Add red and yellow peppers and cucumber and toss gently. In large serving bowl or platter, place lettuce, spinach and red lettuce leaves, well mixed. Arrange chicken mixture on lettuce. Pour lime-soy mixture into frypan and bring to a boil. Remove from heat and drizzle over chicken. Makes 4 servings.

Iola Egle, McCook, NE

Chinese Chicken Rice Salad

4 boneless, skinless chicken breasts	1 can (8 oz.) sliced water chestnuts, drained
2 tablespoons soy sauce	1 cup chopped green onions
2 tablespoons sesame oil	
1 teaspoon salt	1 cup chopped celery
½ teaspoon pepper	1 cup chopped almonds
2 packages (6 oz.) long grain and wild rice mix, cooked according to package directions	1 cup red seedless grapes
	½ cup raisins
	Dressing: recipe follows
	lettuce leaves
1 can (ll oz.) mandarin oranges, drained	1 can Chinese noodles

In small dish, mix together soy sauce and sesame oil; rub thoroughly on chicken and sprinkle with salt and pepper. In large nonstick frypan over medium heat, sauté chicken about 20 minutes or until fork can be inserted with ease. When cool enough to handle, dice chicken and place in large bowl. Add rice, mandarin oranges, water chestnuts, green onions, celery, nuts, grapes and raisins; toss to mix well. Add dressing, continuing to toss. Chill in refrigerator at least l5 minutes. Line large platter with lettuce leaves, place chicken mixture on top and surround with Chinese noodles. Makes 8 servings.

Dressing: In medium bowl, mix together 4 tablespoon sugar, 2 teaspoons salt, ½ cup salad oil, 6 tablespoons vinegar, 1 teaspoon cracked black pepper and 2 tablespoons sesame oil.

Karen O'Brien, Laughlin, NV

Plantation Pecan Chicken

4 boneless, skinless chicken breast halves

½ cup ground pecans

½ cup plain bread crumbs

½ teaspoon salt

¼ cup grated Gruyère cheese

1 tablespoon chopped fresh tarragon

3 tablespoons butter

1 jar (6 oz.) chunky peach preserves

½ cup bottled mild salsa

1 tablespoon capers, rinsed and drained

4 canned Elberta peach halves, drained

½ cup sour cream

4 watercress sprigs

Place chicken between two sheets plastic wrap and gently pound to ¼-inch thickness. In shallow dish, mix together pecans, bread crumbs, salt, cheese and tarragon. In frypan, place butter and melt over low heat. Remove from heat and leave in pan to cool slightly. Dip chicken, one piece at a time, first in butter and then in pecan mixture. Arrange chicken on large nonstick baking pan. Place in 450°F. oven and bake about 15 minutes or until fork can be inserted in chicken with ease. In small saucepan, place peach preserves, salsa and capers. Cook, stirring, to heat through, about 4 minutes. Arrange chicken on serving platter and spoon sauce on top. Fill peach halves with scoop of sour cream and place beside chicken. Garnish with watercress sprigs. Makes 4 servings.

Vivianne Marcotte, Hampton, NH

Buffalo Chicken Supper in a Sub

1	pound chicken breast tenders	¾	cup sliced cucumbers
1	teaspoon garlic powder	½	cup bottled ranch dressing, chilled
1	teaspoon chili powder	4	long sub buns, split
½	teaspoon paprika	4	red bibb lettuce leaves
2	tablespoons flour	2	stalks celery, sliced in strips
1	tablespoon olive oil		
2	tablespoons bottled hot sauce	4	tablespoons crumbled bleu cheese
¾	cup sliced red onion		

In plastic bag, mix together garlic powder, chili powder, paprika and flour; add chicken and turn to coat. In large nonstick frypan, place olive oil over medium-high heat. Add chicken and cook, turning, about 7 minutes or until fork can be inserted with ease. Drizzle hot sauce over chicken, toss to coat; set aside. In medium bowl, mix together onion, cucumber and ranch dressing. Inside each bun, place 1 lettuce leaf and top with chicken and celery; spoon onion-cucumber mixture on top. Sprinkle with bleu cheese. Makes 4 servings.

Gloria Piantek, Skillman, NJ

Lime-Garlic Chicken with Guacamole Noodles

1   pound boneless, skinless chicken breast, cubed

1   teaspoon garlic powder

⅔   cup lime wine cooler

1½ tablespoons olive oil

2   tablespoons flour

½   teaspoon salt

⅛   teaspoon pepper

3   cups noodles, cooked according to package directions

4   tablespoons prepared guacamole

2   tablespoons light sour cream

4   tablespoons shredded Monterey Jack cheese

lime wedges

avocado slices

Place chicken in medium bowl and sprinkle with garlic powder. Add wine cooler, cover and refrigerate at least 30 minutes. Using colander, thoroughly drain marinade from chicken. Mix together flour, salt and pepper; add chicken, turning to coat well. In large frypan over medium-high heat, place olive oil. Add chicken and stir-fry about 4 minutes or until fork can be inserted with ease. Drain noodles and mix with guacamole and sour cream; arrange on serving platter and top with chicken. Sprinkle with cheese. Garnish with lime wedges and thin slices of avocado (dipped in lemon to avoid discoloring). Makes 4 servings.

Joan Dean, Corrales, NM

Chicken with Brie, Apricot Preserves and Almonds

4	boneless, skinless chicken breast halves	8	tablespoons apricot preserves
2	tablespoons olive oil	½	cup sliced almonds
8	ounces brie cheese, quartered		parsley sprigs

Place chicken between 2 pieces plastic wrap and gently pound to ¼-inch thickness. In large frypan, place olive oil over medium heat. Add chicken and cook about 3 minutes on each side or until brown and fork can be inserted with ease. Arrange chicken in single layer in baking dish. Top each piece with a quarter of brie cheese and 2 tablespoons apricot preserves. Sprinkle with almonds and place in 400°F. oven until cheese is bubbly, about 7 minutes. Garnish with parsley sprigs. Makes 4 servings.

Tracey Wolpert, Cooperstown, NY

Tortilla-Pecan Crusted Chicken

4	boneless, skinless chicken breast halves	½	cup finely crushed tortilla chips
8	sun-dried tomatoes (not oil packed)	½	cup finely chopped pecans
1	cup boiling water	1	tablespoon slightly beaten egg white
	Southwestern Paste: recipe follows		lettuce leaves
3	ounces Monterey Jack cheese with jalapeno peppers, sliced in thin strips	2	red jalapeno peppers, cut in rings

In small bowl, place sun-dried tomatoes. Add water and soak about 30 minutes or until soft; drain, pat dry and slice. On thicker side of each chicken breast half, cut a horizontal pocket, being careful not to cut through opposite side. Brush inside of pockets with 1 tablespoon of Southwestern Paste. Stuff each breast half with equal portions of sun dried tomatoes and cheese; press edges firmly to seal. Brush remaining Southwestern Paste on both sides of chicken. In large shallow dish, place tortilla chips, pecans and egg white; stir to mix well. Add chicken to crumb mixture, pressing to adhere coating. Arrange chicken on nonstick jelly roll pan and place in 400°F. oven for about 25 minutes or until fork can be inserted with ease. Line serving dish with lettuce leaves. Arrange chicken on lettuce and top with jalapeno pepper rings. Makes 4 servings.

Southwestern Paste: In small bowl, mix together 3 tablespoons hot honey mustard, 1½ teaspoons chili powder, 1½ teaspoons dried cilantro, ¾ teaspoon ground cumin, ¾ teaspoon dried oregano, ½ teaspoon salt and 2 small cloves garlic (pressed).

Frances Andrews, Wilson, NC

Valley Chicken

4   boneless, skinless chicken breast halves

2   tablespoons soy sauce

2   tablespoons light bottled Italian salad dressing

6   tablespoons catsup

½   teaspoon dill weed

½   teaspoon garlic powder

½   teaspoon Greek seasoning

½   cup white wine

2   tablespoons cooking oil

2   tablespoons butter

fresh dill sprigs

In medium bowl, mix together soy sauce, Italian dressing, catsup, dill weed, garlic powder, Greek seasoning and wine; set aside. In large frypan over medium-high heat, place cooking oil and butter. Add chicken and lightly brown on both sides. Cover and cook about 10 minutes more or until fork can be inserted in chicken with ease. Drain pan and pour sauce mixture over chicken. Cover and simmer about 10 minutes more. Arrange chicken on platter and pour sauce over top. Garnish with dill sprigs. Makes 4 servings.

Clarence Lind, Fargo, ND

Oven-Fried Chicken Madras

4   boneless, skinless
    chicken breast halves

⅓   cup plain nonfat
    yogurt

1   teaspoon curry powder

½   cup finely chopped
    pistachios

½   cup bread crumbs

2   tablespoons coarsely
    chopped mint leaves

½   teaspoon salt

¼   teaspoon pepper

    Yogurt-Pistachio Sauce:
    recipe follows

    cilantro sprigs

    mint sprigs

In shallow bowl, mix together yogurt and curry powder. On sheet of wax paper, mix together pistachios, bread crumbs, mint, salt and pepper. Dip chicken in yogurt mixture, then roll in pistachio mixture, coating well. Lightly coat chicken with cooking spray; arrange in baking pan sprayed with cooking spray. Place in 400°F. oven for about 30 minutes or until fork can be inserted in chicken with ease. Garnish with cilantro and mint sprigs; pass Yogurt-Pistachio Sauce. Makes 4 servings.

Yogurt-Pistachio Sauce: In small bowl, mix together 1 container (8 oz.) plain nonfat yogurt, 3 tablespoons toasted chopped pistachios, ¼ cup chopped cilantro leaves, 2 tablespoons chopped mint leaves, 1 teaspoon fresh lemon juice, ¼ teaspoon salt and ⅛ teaspoon hot pepper sauce.

Annette Erbeck, Mason, OH

Mexican Chicken Salad

2 whole boneless, skinless chicken breasts, halved

⅔ cup fresh lime juice

⅔ cup garlic flavored olive oil

⅓ cup chopped cilantro

½ cup chopped shallots

½ teaspoon salt

1 cup crushed salsa flavored tortilla chips

2 cups shredded Napa cabbage

2 cups shredded spinach

1 can (15 oz.) corn with peppers

1 red bell pepper, julienned

2 plum tomatoes, chopped

1 avocado, peeled and diced

½ cup crumbled feta cheese

Cut chicken crosswise into ½-inch pieces and place in bowl. In medium bowl, whisk together lime juice, olive oil, cilantro, shallots and salt. Reserve ½ of mixture for dressing and pour remainder over chicken, tossing to coat. On piece of wax paper, place tortilla chips. Roll chicken pieces in chips, coating well. Place chicken in single layer on greased baking sheet. Bake in 400°F. oven for about 20 minutes, or until brown and fork can be inserted in chicken with ease. In large bowl, mix together cabbage, spinach, corn, red pepper, tomatoes, avocado and feta cheese. Pour reserved dressing over mixture and toss gently. Place cabbage mixture on platter or in large shallow salad bowl and arrange chicken on top. Makes 4 servings.

Jeanette Atwood, Oklahoma City, OK

Sunny Chicken and Black Beans

4   boneless, skinless chicken breast halves

¼   cup finely chopped onion

1   clove garlic, minced

8   mushrooms, quartered

¼   cup white wine

½   teaspoon dried basil

½   teaspoon salt

¼   teaspoon pepper

½   cup sun-dried tomatoes

1   cup hot water

1   tablespoon cornstarch

½   cup chicken broth

¼   cup nonfat sour cream

1   can (15 oz.) black beans, drained

    basil sprigs

With palm of hand or meat mallet, slightly flatten chicken breasts. Spray large frypan with cooking spray and place over medium heat. Add onion, garlic and mushrooms and sauté about 5 minutes or until mushrooms are lightly browned. Push vegetables to edge of pan and add chicken, wine, basil, salt and pepper; cook over medium-low heat about 20 minutes, turning chicken once. Soak sun-dried tomatoes in hot water for 10 minutes; drain and dice. In small bowl, place cornstarch; add chicken broth, stirring to dissolve. Remove chicken from pan and keep warm. To vegetables remaining in pan, add cornstarch, sour cream and black beans. Heat, stirring, about 3 minutes or until slightly thickened. Arrange chicken on serving platter, spoon black bean sauce on top and sprinkle with sun-dried tomatoes. Garnish with basil sprigs. Makes 4 servings.

Laurie Farquhar, Tualatin, OR

Thai Chicken with Basil

4	boneless, skinless chicken breast halves, cut in thin strips	2	teaspoons grated lime zest
1	teaspoon oil	3½	tablespoons oyster sauce
1¼	cups chopped shiitake mushrooms	½	cup chopped basil
2	large garlic cloves, minced	1	cup jasmine rice, cooked according to package directions
⅛	teaspoon hot red pepper flakes		basil leaves

In large nonstick frypan over medium heat, place oil. Add mushrooms, garlic and pepper flakes; cook, stirring, about 3 minutes and remove from pan. To frypan, add chicken and cook about 3 minutes or until fork can be inserted with ease. Return mushroom mixture to pan; add lime zest, oyster sauce and basil and heat through, about 3 minutes more. Place cooked rice on serving platter, top with chicken mixture and garnish with basil leaves. Makes 4 servings.

Marian Nowell, Philadelphia, PA

Pistachio Crusted Chicken Schnitzel

4	boneless, skinless chicken breast halves, julienned	1/2	teaspoon salt
1	cup coarsely chopped pistachio nuts	1/2	teaspoon pepper
1/2	teaspoon grated lemon zest	2	egg whites, slightly beaten
1	teaspoon brown sugar	3	tablespoons canola oil
2	tablespoons flour		Cucumber Sauce: recipe follows
			lemon slices

In large bowl, place chicken. Add pistachio nuts, lemon zest, brown sugar, flour, salt, pepper and egg whites; stir to mix well and thoroughly coat chicken. Place oil in large nonstick frypan over medium heat; add chicken mixture and stir to separate chicken strips. Sauté, stirring frequently, about 12 minutes or until coating is light brown and fork can be inserted in chicken with ease. On large serving platter, place Cucumber Sauce in container with small ladle. Arrange chicken around sauce and garnish with lemon slices. Makes 4 servings.

Cucumber Sauce: In blender or food processor, coarsely chop 1 medium cucumber, peeled. In saucepan over low heat, place 1 cup sour cream and 1 tablespoon milk; heat about 2 minutes or until slightly bubbly. Stir in cucumber and sprinkle with 1 teaspoon sesame seed and 1/4 teaspoon paprika.

Beverly Reinert, Barrington, RI

Chicken Messina

2	whole boneless, skinless chicken breasts, cut in 1½-inch pieces	4	quarts boiling water
1	teaspoon salt, divided	1	cup orzo
½	teaspoon freshly ground pepper, divided	2	tablespoons butter
2	tablespoons flour	3	tablespoons minced parsley
2	tablespoons olive oil	¼	cup balsamic vinegar
1	clove garlic, minced	1	tablespoon capers, drained
2	cups chicken stock, divided	6	tablespoons crumbled feta cheese
		½	Bosc pear, cored and sliced

Sprinkle chicken with ½ teaspoon of the salt and ¼ teaspoon of the pepper; dust chicken with flour. In large frypan, place oil over medium-high heat. Add chicken and sauté about 3 minutes per side or until browned and fork tender. Remove chicken from frypan and discard oil. To frypan, add garlic and sauté 10 seconds. Add 1 cup of the chicken stock and boil 1 minute, stirring to scrap up brown bits. Return chicken to pan, cover, lower heat and simmer 10 minutes. In large saucepan, place water and orzo; cook until al dente, about 9 minutes. Drain, add butter and parsley and toss. Add remaining ½ teaspoon salt and ¼ teaspoon pepper. Remove cover from frypan containing chicken, increase heat to high and add remaining cup of chicken stock, vinegar and capers. Cook about 8 minutes, stirring, until consistency is syrupy. Place orzo on serving platter, top with chicken mixture, sprinkle with feta cheese and garnish with pear slices. Makes 4 servings.

David Scaturo, Columbia, SC

Easy Crunchy Baked Chicken

1 cut-up chicken, skin removed	½ teaspoon salt
2 tablespoons margarine	¼ teaspoon freshly ground pepper
1½ cups oat bran cereal	½ cup lowfat yogurt
3 tablespoons oat bran	1 tablespoon spicy mustard
1 tablespoon finely chopped fresh sage	coriander sprigs

In baking dish, place margarine and melt in 350°F. oven. In plastic bag, mix together oat bran cereal, oat bran, sage, salt and pepper; crush with rolling pin and place on wax paper. In small bowl, mix together yogurt and mustard; brush on chicken and roll chicken in oat bran mixture to coat well. Arrange chicken in baking dish with margarine and place in oven for 1 hour. Garnish with coriander. Makes 4 servings.

Sandra Hansen, Winner, SD

Chicken Greek

8	boneless, skinless chicken breast halves	4	pepperoncini peppers, diced
3	tablespoons olive oil, divided	1	cup diced tomatoes
½	teaspoon salt	8	ounces feta cheese
¼	teaspoon pepper	½	pound herb seasoned stuffing
2	teaspoons dried cilantro	2	eggs, beaten
2	garlic cloves, finely minced		cherry tomatoes
24	black olives, sliced		carrot strips
⅓	cup diced onion		black olive slices
			cilantro sprigs

Place chicken between 2 sheets of plastic wrap and flatten to ¼-inch thickness. Brush with 2 tablespoons of the olive oil and sprinkle with salt, pepper and cilantro. In small saucepan, place remaining 1 tablespoon olive oil over medium heat. Add garlic, olives, onion and peppers; sauté just until tender, about 2 minutes. Divide mixture into 8 equal parts and spread in center of each chicken piece. Top each with 2 tablespoons diced tomatoes and ⅛ of feta cheese. Fold chicken around the mixture; secure with picks. Place stuffing in shallow pan and in another dish, place eggs. Dip each chicken roll first in egg, then in stuffing. Line baking pan with foil and arrange chicken in single layer. Bake in 350°F. oven about 30 minutes or until fork can be inserted in chicken with ease. Garnish with cherry tomatoes, carrot strips, black olive slices and cilantro sprigs. Makes 8 servings.

Lori Cook, Murfreesboro, TN

Mango Colada Chicken with Ginger Fruit

12 medium chicken thighs, skinned	1 teaspoon grated gingerroot
1½ cups cubed half ripe mango	1 teaspoon allspice
¼ cup rum	curly lettuce leaves
2 tablespoons sweetened coconut cream	1 tablespoon toasted sesame seed
¼ cup soy sauce	Ginger Fruit: recipe follows

In food processor, place mango and purée. Add rum, coconut cream, soy sauce, gingerroot and allspice. Coat chicken with mango mixture and place in baking pan. Bake at 400°F., uncovered, about 50 minutes, turning frequently, until fork can be inserted in chicken with ease. (Increase heat to reduce liquid if necessary toward end of cooking.) Line round serving platter with lettuce. Place chicken in center, sprinkle with sesame seed and arrange Ginger Fruit around chicken. Makes 6 servings.

Ginger Fruit: In large bowl, mix together 4 tablespoons sweetened coconut cream and ½ teaspoon grated gingerroot. Add 2 cups cubed and peeled ripe mango, 1 pint strawberries (hulled) and 2 cups seedless purple grapes. Toss to mix well.

Loanne Chiu, Fort Worth, TX

Dilly Chicken

6   boneless, skinless chicken breast halves

2   tablespoons cooking oil

1   tablespoon fresh lemon juice

½   teaspoon lemon pepper

½   cup peeled and chopped cucumber

1   tablespoon chopped parsley

2   teaspoons chopped chives

¼   teaspoon dried dill weed

1   cup sour cream

½   teaspoon sugar

    parsley sprigs

    lemon twists

Between 2 sheets of plastic wrap, place chicken and flatten to ½-inch thickness. In large frypan, place oil, lemon juice and lemon pepper over medium heat. Add chicken and cook about 10 minutes, turning once, until chicken is brown and fork can be inserted with ease. Remove chicken to platter and keep warm. To frypan, add cucumber, parsley, chives and dill weed; cook 2 minutes, stirring. Add sour cream and sugar and continue to cook about 2 more minutes to heat through. Spoon cucumber mixture over chicken and garnish with parsley and lemon twists. Makes 6 servings.

Carol Bartholomew, Salt Lake City, UT

Chicken Fans with Black Bean Risotto

4	boneless, skinless chicken breast halves	1	cup prepared salsa, warmed
2	tablespoons lime juice	½	cup finely shredded Colby Jack cheese
1	teaspoon chili powder		cilantro sprigs
½	teaspoon cumin		
	Black Bean Risotto: recipe follows		

Brush chicken on all sides with lime juice. Sprinkle with chili powder and cumin and place on broiler pan. Broil about 6 inches from heat about 5 minutes on each side or until fork can be inserted in chicken with ease. To serve, divide Black Bean Risotto among 4 individual serving plates. Thinly slice chicken ¾ way through and place on top of risotto, fanning out slices. Spoon salsa across center of chicken and sprinkle with cheese. Garnish with cilantro sprigs. Makes 4 servings.

Black Bean Risotto: In medium saucepan over medium heat, melt 1 tablespoon butter. Add ½ cup Arborio rice and sauté 1 minute. Add ¼ cup dry white wine and cook, stirring, until liquid is absorbed. In small saucepan, warm 2 cups reduced sodium chicken broth; add to rice, ½ cup at a time, stirring after each addition, until moisture is almost absorbed. Remove from heat and stir in ½ cup drained canned black beans, ¼ cup shredded Colby Jack cheese, 2 teaspoons chopped cilantro, 1 tablespoon butter, ½ teaspoon salt and ¼ teaspoon pepper.

Lori Welander, Shelburne, VT

Chicken, Apple and Cheese Bundles

4 boneless, skinless chicken breast halves, chopped in bite-size chunks

1 tablespoon olive oil

1 large onion, chopped

2 large Golden Delicious apples, peeled and diced

1½ cups grated smoked Gouda cheese

½ teaspoon salt

¼ teaspoon pepper

¼ cup chopped walnuts

3 large rolls refrigerated commercial crescent roll dough

In large frypan, place olive oil over medium heat. Add onion and sauté until tender, about 2 minutes. Add chicken and stir-fry about 5 minutes or until fork can be inserted with ease. Remove chicken and onion to large bowl; stir in apples, cheese, salt, pepper and walnuts. On 1 crescent roll section, place 1 tablespoon of the chicken-apple mixture. Fold corners across filling and pinch sides to seal. Repeat with remaining dough and filling. Arrange bundles on baking sheet sprayed with nonstick cooking spray and place in 350°F. oven for about 15 minutes or until brown and bubbly. Makes 24 bundles.

Amy Terzino, Earlysville, VA

Sweet Curry Chicken Melon Salad

4	boneless, skinless chicken breast halves	1	teaspoon mild curry powder
¼	cup water	1	teaspoon ground ginger
4	cups cubed mixed melon (cantaloupe, honeydew, red and yellow watermelon)	1	tablespoon fresh lime juice
		4	butter lettuce leaves
		4	red leaf lettuce leaves
1	sweet red pepper, julienned	1	avocado, peeled and thinly sliced
1	cup red seedless grapes, divided	2	limes; 1 cut in wedges, 1 tablespoon zest
¾	cup mayonnaise	1	cup chopped walnuts
2	tablespoons brown sugar		
4	tablespoons finely chopped cilantro, divided		

In large nonstick pan, place water over medium-high heat. Add chicken, cover and cook about 15 minutes or until fork can be inserted in chicken with ease. Cool chicken and cut into cubes. In colander, mix together melon, red pepper and grapes, reserving 12 of the grapes for garnish. In large bowl, mix together mayonnaise, sugar, 2 tablespoons of the cilantro, curry, ginger and lime juice. Add chicken and gently toss to coat well. On serving plate, arrange lettuce, alternating butter and red lettuce leaves. Place fruit mixture around edge of dish and chicken mixture in center. Sprinkle with remaining 2 tablespoons cilantro, lime zest and walnuts. Garnish with avocado slices, lime wedges and clusters of reserved grapes. Makes 6 servings.

Cheryl McAtee, Vancouver, WA

Chicken Rolls with Cranberry Filling

4 boneless, skinless chicken breast halves	1 cup crushed herb stuffing mix, divided
1/3 cup orange juice	1/2 teaspoon ground sage
2/3 cup plus 2 tablespoons dried cranberries, divided	1/2 teaspoon white pepper
5 tablespoons margarine, divided	3 tablespoons honey mustard
1/4 cup chopped celery	tomato rosettes
1/4 cup chopped green onion	parsley sprigs

Between two sheets plastic wrap, place chicken breasts and flatten with mallet or palm of hand. In small saucepan, place orange juice and heat over medium heat. Add cranberries, cover and set aside to soften. In another saucepan, place 2 tablespoons of the margarine and melt over medium heat. Add celery and onion and sauté about 2 minutes. To 1/3 cup of the stuffing mix, add sage; stir into celery-onion mixture and add 2/3 cup of the cranberries. Sprinkle chicken with pepper and coat with mustard. Spoon cranberry mixture in center of each piece, roll chicken over filling and fasten with wooden picks. Melt remaining 3 tablespoons margarine and dip each chicken roll, first in margarine and then in remaining 2/3 cup crushed stuffing. Place chicken on baking pan lined with foil and sprayed with vegetable spray. Bake, uncovered, in 350°F. oven about 30 minutes or until fork can be inserted in chicken with ease. Garnish with tomato rosettes and parsley; sprinkle chicken with remaining 2 tablespoons cranberries. Makes 4 servings.

Carolyn Blakemore, Fairmont, WV

Braised Chicken Breasts with Plum Sauce

6   boneless, skinless chicken breast halves
3   tablespoons olive oil, divided
2   tablespoons fresh lemon juice
1   clove garlic, minced
1   teaspoon soy sauce
½   teaspoon dried basil
½   teaspoon dried oregano
½   teaspoon dried rosemary, crumbled
¼   teaspoon salt
¼   teaspoon pepper
1   tablespoon butter
    Plum Sauce: recipe follows
    parsley sprigs

In large shallow dish, place chicken. In small bowl, mix together 2 tablespoons of the olive oil, lemon juice, garlic, soy sauce, basil, oregano, rosemary, salt and pepper. Pour over chicken and marinate in refrigerator about 30 minutes, turning chicken occasionally. In large frypan, place remaining 1 tablespoon olive oil and butter over medium heat. Remove chicken from marinade, add to pan and sauté, turning once, about 15 minutes or until chicken is brown on both sides and fork can be inserted with ease. Arrange chicken on warm serving platter and spoon Plum Sauce around edges. Garnish with parsley sprigs. Makes 6 servings.

Plum Sauce: Drain 1 can (15 oz.) whole purple plums, remove pits and chop coarsely; reserve 2 tablespoons of the syrup. In heavy saucepan, place plums, reserved syrup, 2 tablespoons butter, ½ cup finely chopped onion, ¼ cup brown sugar, ¼ cup chili sauce, 2 tablespoons soy sauce, 1 teaspoon ground ginger, 2 teaspoons lemon juice and ½ cup chopped walnuts. Simmer over low heat, uncovered, 5 minutes, stirring occasionally.

Ellen Marie Anders, Big Bend, WI

Garlic Dilled Chicken Mirage

4 boneless, skinless chicken breast halves, cut in bite-size pieces

2 tablespoons extra light olive oil

¾ cup diced onion

10 garlic cloves, minced

1 can (16 oz.) chicken broth

3 cups fresh broccoli flowerets, chopped

3 carrots, peeled and cut in thin strips

6 mushrooms, chopped

⅓ cup marinated sun-dried tomatoes packed in oil, drained and chopped

2 teaspoons dried dill

1 teaspoon dried parsley

1 teaspoon pepper

1½ tablespoons cornstarch, dissolved in ¼ cup cold water

1 package (8 oz.) extra wide egg noodles, cooked according to package directions

In large saucepan, place olive oil and heat over medium-high temperature. Add chicken and onion and stir-fry until chicken is cooked through, about 4 minutes. Stir in garlic; then add chicken broth, broccoli, carrots, mushrooms, sun-dried tomatoes, dill, parsley and pepper. Cover and cook about 5 minutes more or until vegetables are tender crisp. Add cornstarch and cook, uncovered, until slightly thickened, about 2 minutes more. Place noodles on serving dish and arrange chicken mixture over top. Makes 4 servings.

Sally Ferris, Gillette, WY

Host State Recipes

South Carolina is known for its good food and warm hospitality. Since the early days of this nation, chicken has been a favorite on dinner tables in that state from its Low Country to the Upstate. Here is a sampling of how chicken is cooked in the state that hosted the 42nd National Chicken Cooking Contest.

Marinated Breast of Chicken with Orange Barbecue Sauce

8   boneless, skinless chicken breast halves

1   can (6 oz.) frozen orange juice, thawed, undiluted

1/4   cup soy sauce

1/2   teaspoon pepper

1   clove garlic, minced

1   tablespoon ground ginger

   Orange Barbecue Sauce: recipe follows

In small bowl, mix together orange juice concentrate, soy sauce, pepper, garlic and ginger. Pour over chicken and marinate in refrigerator about 3 hours or overnight, turning occasionally. Drain chicken and place in single layer in shallow roasting pan sprayed with nonstick cooking spray. Bake in 375°F. oven (or cook on prepared grill) about 30 minutes or until fork can be inserted in chicken with ease. During final 5 minutes of cooking, spoon Orange Barbecue Sauce over chicken. Makes 8 servings.

Orange Barbecue Sauce: In medium saucepan, mix together 1/3 cup orange juice, 1/2 cup catsup, 1/2 cup chili sauce, 3 tablespoons molasses, 3 tablespoons red wine vinegar, 1 tablespoon Worcestershire sauce, 1/2 teaspoon garlic powder, 1/4 teaspoon ground cloves and 1/2 teaspoon ground red pepper. Place over medium-low heat and cook 10 minutes, stirring occasionally. Cool.

—Recipe of Mary Wood Beasley, wife of South Carolina Governor David Beasley.

Ginger Pear Chicken

8	boneless, skinless chicken breast halves	4	tablespoons vinegar
¼	cup butter	5	tablespoons soy sauce
½	teaspoon salt	1	tablespoon ground ginger
¼	teaspoon pepper		
2	cans (16 oz.) pear halves	4	tablespoons cornstarch
2	cups ginger ale	½	cup water
½	cup brown sugar	½	cup toasted pecan halves

In large frypan, melt butter over medium heat. Add chicken and cook, turning, about 5 minutes or until lightly browned; sprinkle with salt and pepper. Drain pears and reserve liquid. In medium bowl, mix together ginger ale, brown sugar, vinegar, soy sauce and ginger. Add to chicken along with reserved pear juice. Simmer about 1 hour; remove chicken to warm plate. In small bowl, mix together cornstarch and water; add to liquid in frypan, stirring. When sauce thickens, return chicken to pan and add pears and toasted pecans. Heat through. Makes 8 servings.

—Adapted from *Uptown Down South*, cookbook of Junior League of Greenville, South Carolina.

Roast Breast of Chicken with Cherry Sage Bread Pudding

4	boneless chicken breasts	1	tablespoon diced celery
1	pint cream	1	tablespoon diced onion
4	eggs	1	tablespoon toasted pecan pieces
1	teaspoon salt	1	teaspoon chopped fresh sage
1	teaspoon white pepper		
4	stale croissants, diced	½	cup dried cherries
⅓	cup rendered chicken fat, divided	½	cup diced apple

In medium bowl, mix together cream, eggs, salt and pepper; set aside. In frypan, place ½ of rendered chicken fat over medium-high heat. Add diced croissants and toast lightly; remove from pan and set aside. Add remaining chicken fat to pan and stir in celery, onion, pecan pieces, sage, cherries and apple; cook, stirring, until ingredients soften, about 2 minutes. Put this mixture into well greased timbales or coffee cups, filling about half full. Pour egg mixture on top and let soak 1 minute; pour off any excess. Place individual molds in pan of water and bake in 325°F. oven about 35 minutes. In frypan, sauté chicken, skin side down; turn and continue cooking about 2 minutes more. Place chicken in 325°F. oven and cook about 10 minutes or until fork can be inserted with ease. Remove chicken from oven, let rest 10 minutes and slice. Remove bread pudding from cup and arrange on plate with chicken slices around it. Makes 4 servings.

—Recipe of Chef Ken Vedrenski,
Woodlands Resort and Inn's
Five-Diamond Restaurant,
Summerville, South Carolina.

Crab Stuffed Chicken Breasts

8 boneless, skinless chicken breast halves

¼ teaspoon salt

1 egg, beaten

1 cup herb seasoned stuffing

½ can (10¾ oz.) cream of mushroom soup

1 can (6½ oz.) crabmeat, drained

¼ cup chopped green pepper

1 tablespoon lemon juice

2 teaspoons Worcestershire sauce

1 teaspoon prepared mustard

melted butter

crispy rice cereal, crushed

garlic powder (optional)

Sprinkle chicken with salt and flatten by pounding. In small bowl, mix together egg, stuffing, mushroom soup, crabmeat, green pepper, lemon juice, Worcestershire and mustard. Place even portions of mixture on each chicken breast half and roll chicken around stuffing; dip in melted butter and then in crushed cereal. Sprinkle lightly with garlic powder, if desired. Place in 350°F. oven for about 1 hour. Makes 8 servings.

—Adapted from *Putting on the Grits*, cookbook of Junior League of Columbia, South Carolina.

Grandmother's Chicken Croquettes

1 quart chopped, cooked chicken

½ teaspoon salt

¼ teaspoon black pepper

1 quart milk

½ onion, thinly sliced

1 lemon, grated rind only

3 eggs

1 tablespoon chopped parsley

¼ whole nutmeg, grated

⅛ teaspoon red pepper

½ pound butter

1 tablespoon cornstarch

3 tablespoons flour

3 tablespoons milk

bread crumbs

Sprinkle salt and black pepper on chicken. In saucepan, place milk, onion and lemon rind over medium heat; bring almost to a boil. Separate yolk and white of 1 egg, placing white in medium bowl and reserving yolk. To egg white, add 2 remaining eggs, parsley, nutmeg and red pepper. In large saucepan, cream together butter, cornstarch and flour; gradually stir in heated milk-onion mixture and place over medium heat. Stir in egg mixture and when thickened, add chicken. Remove from heat, cool slightly and mold into croquettes, using a large pointed wine glass. Slightly beat reserved egg yolk and add the 3 tablespoons milk. Dip croquettes in egg and roll in bread crumbs. Deep fry in hot oil until browned. Makes 10 servings.

—Adapted from *Charleston Receipts*, cookbook of Junior League of Charleston, South Carolina.

Chicken Liver Stroganoff

1	pound chicken livers	⅛	teaspoon pepper
2	tablespoons butter	1	can (6 oz.) sliced mushrooms, drained
½	cup chopped onion		
2	tablespoons flour	¼	cup sour cream
¼	teaspoon dried oregano		cooked rice
½	teaspoon Worcestershire sauce	8	slices bacon, crisply cooked
½	teaspoon salt		

In large frypan, place butter over medium heat. Add chicken livers and cook about 5 minutes, turning, to brown; remove from pan. To frypan, add onion and sauté until soft, about 2 minutes. Stir in flour, oregano, Worcestershire sauce, salt and pepper. Add mushrooms, sour cream and chicken livers; simmer about 4 minutes but do not boil. Serve over rice and top with crumbled bacon. Makes 6 servings.

—Adapted from *Putting on the Grits*, cookbook of Junior League of Columbia, South Carolina. (Recipe of Mrs. Richard Riley, wife of former Governor of South Carolina, now Secretary of Education in the President's Cabinet.)

Sweet and Sour Chicken

4 boneless, skinless chicken breast halves (or 1 cut-up chicken)	¼ cup chopped bell pepper
½ cup flour	1 teaspoon prepared mustard
½ teaspoon salt	½ teaspoon garlic salt
¼ teaspoon pepper	2 tablespoons soy sauce
½ cup cooking oil	1 tablespoon molasses
1 cup orange juice	1 small can Mandarin orange sections
½ cup chili sauce	

In plastic bag, place flour, salt and pepper. Add chicken and shake to coat well. In frypan, place oil over medium-high heat. Add chicken and brown on both sides, about 5 minutes. Remove chicken to 3-quart casserole. Drain oil from frypan and add orange juice, chili sauce, bell pepper, mustard, garlic salt, soy sauce and molasses. Simmer, stirring, about 5 minutes and pour over chicken; cover casserole with foil. (May be frozen at this point for later cooking.) Place chicken in 350°F. oven and bake, covered, about 55 minutes. Remove foil and top chicken with Mandarin orange sections (more orange juice may be added at this time if thinner sauce is preferred). Return to oven and cook an additional 10 minutes. Serve over rice. Makes 4 servings.

—Recipe of Mrs. Fritz Hollings, wife of the U.S. Senator from South Carolina. Served when President and Mrs. Clinton dined in their home.

Slow Cooked Chicken with Asiago Creamy Grits
(Recipe on page 87)

Cumin Crusted Chicken Borracho Beans and
Braised Mustard Greens (Recipe on page 85)

Sautéed Chicken Breast with Sweet and
Sour Melon Sauce (Recipe on page 80)

Baked Spicy Pineapple Balinese Chicken
(Recipe on page 66)

Previous Winners

Cooks from coast to coast have enjoyed serving winning recipes from the 41st National Chicken Cooking Contest, which was held in Atlanta, Georgia. Here is the $25,000 prize winner and four other recipes chosen by a panel of judges as the best prepared at that Cook-Off in 1995.

Baked Spicy Pineapple Balinese Chicken

(Pictured in color section)

4 boneless, skinless chicken breast halves	Spicy Pineapple Sauce: recipe follows
3 tablespoons Dijon mustard	red bell pepper strips
½ cup gingersnap crumbs	basil sprigs

Between two sheets plastic wrap, place chicken and gently pound to uniform thickness. Brush chicken with mustard. In shallow dish, place gingersnap crumbs. Add chicken, 1 piece at a time, dredging to coat. In nonstick sprayed shallow baking dish, place chicken and refrigerate 20 minutes. Place chicken in 350°F. oven and bake about 20 minutes or until fork can be inserted in chicken with ease. On 4 individual plates, spoon ¼ of Spicy Pineapple Sauce. Add chicken breast half to each plate. Garnish with red bell pepper strips and basil sprigs. Makes 4 servings.

Spicy Pineapple Sauce: In frypan, place 1 tablespoon peanut oil and heat to medium temperature. Add 1 minced garlic clove and 1 red onion, chopped. Sauté about 2 minutes. Stir in ¼ cup seasoned rice vinegar and 1 can (8 oz.) crushed pineapple, juice included. Add ¼ teaspoon allspice, ¼ teaspoon red pepper flakes and 2½ teaspoons Dijon mustard. Heat, stirring, about 4 minutes or until bubbly and slightly thickened. In blender container, place pineapple mixture and purée until smooth; keep warm. Just before serving, stir in 2 tablespoons finely chopped basil and ¼ cup diced red bell pepper.

Mary Louise Lever, Georgia

Gingered Jamaican Jerk Chicken

4	boneless, skinless chicken breast halves	¼	teaspoon cayenne pepper
1	tablespoon chili powder	3	tablespoons olive oil
1½	teaspoons curry powder	⅓	cup small-diced fresh ginger
1½	teaspoons thyme leaves	6	large slices red onion
1	teaspoon paprika	2	tablespoons butter
1	teaspoon coarsely ground black pepper	3	tablespoons lemon juice
½	teaspoon cumin	3	Granny Smith apples, peeled, cored and thinly sliced
½	teaspoon granulated garlic	⅓	cup light brown sugar
½	teaspoon salt		parsley sprigs
¼	teaspoon allspice		

In small bowl, make jerk seasoning by mixing together chili powder, curry powder, thyme leaves, paprika, pepper, cumin, garlic, salt, allspice and cayenne pepper. Sprinkle on chicken, coating both sides. In large frypan, place oil and heat to medium-high temperature. Add chicken and ginger; cook about 10 minutes or until fork can be inserted in chicken with ease. Remove chicken from frypan and keep warm. In same frypan, place red onion slices and cook, turning once, about 3 minutes or until tender. Remove onion from frypan and set aside. In frypan, place butter and melt; add lemon juice and apples. Sauté until apples begin to soften. Add brown sugar and cook until liquid is reduced and thickens. Arrange onion slices on serving plate; top with chicken and apple mixture. Garnish with parsley. Makes 4 servings.

Diane Lentz, Kentucky

Jalapeno Tex-Mex Chicken Salad

4 boneless, skinless chicken breast halves

Jalapeno Cream Dressing: recipe follows

2 teaspoons taco seasoning

1 teaspoon garlic pepper

1 tablespoon vegetable oil

⅔ cup canned black beans, rinsed and drained

½ cup canned corn, drained

¼ cup mild picante sauce

1 tablespoon chopped green onion tops

⅔ cup chopped, seeded tomato

4 cup bag prepared mixed salad greens

8 thin slices jalapeno pepper

1 plum tomato, cut in wedges

cilantro sprigs

Prepare Jalapeno Cream Dressing; set aside. In small bowl, mix taco seasoning and garlic pepper; sprinkle on both sides of chicken. In large frypan, place oil and heat to medium temperature. Add chicken and cook about 12 minutes or until brown on both sides and fork can be inserted with ease. Remove chicken from frypan and set aside. In frypan, place black beans, corn and picante sauce. Cook just to heat through; remove from heat. Stir in green onion and tomato. Arrange salad greens on serving platter. Cut each chicken breast in crosswise slices (do not separate) and fan slices. Place on top of salad greens and top each chicken breast with 1 tablespoon Jalapeno Cream Dressing and 2 slices jalapeno pepper. Spoon warm bean mixture around chicken. Garnish with tomato wedges and cilantro. Pass extra dressing. Makes 4 servings.

Jalapeno Cream Dressing: In small bowl, mix together ½ cup jalapeno pepper jelly, ½ cup sour cream, 1 tablespoon fresh lime juice and 1 tablespoon minced fresh cilantro.

Jeanne Holt, Minnesota

Key Lime Thai Chicken

6	boneless, skinless chicken breast halves	1	teaspoon dried mint
½	cup Key lime juice	½	teaspoon crushed red pepper flakes
¼	cup vegetable oil	½	teaspoon freshly ground black pepper
1	tablespoon honey		cilantro sprigs
4	garlic cloves, minced		Key Lime Thai Cucumber Salsa: recipe follows
¼	cup chopped green onion, white and green parts included		
½	cup chopped fresh cilantro		

In shallow glass dish, place chicken. In small bowl, make marinade by whisking together lime juice, oil, honey, garlic, onion, cilantro, mint, red pepper and black pepper. Pour over chicken, turning to coat. Refrigerate and marinate at least 15 minutes. Remove chicken from marinade. Place chicken on broiler pan 6 inches from heat. Broil, turning, about 10 minutes or until fork can be inserted in chicken with ease. Garnish with cilantro sprigs and serve with Key Lime Thai Cucumber Salsa. Makes 6 servings.

Key Lime Thai Cucumber Salsa: In medium bowl, mix together ½ cup Key lime juice, ¼ cup vegetable oil, ¼ cup sugar, ½ teaspoon salt, 2 teaspoons Thai chili sauce, ½ cup chopped green onions, 2 peeled and diced small cucumbers and ¼ cup chopped fresh cilantro. Cover and refrigerate. Before serving, sprinkle with ¼ cup finely chopped roasted peanuts.

Edwina Gadsby, Montana

Thai Chicken Thigh Kabobs

8   boneless, skinless chicken thighs
½   cup hot garlic soy sauce
¼   cup packed brown sugar
¼   cup catsup
2   tablespoons fresh lime juice
1   large shallot, chopped
1   tablespoon peanut butter

1   large sweet onion
1   each; large seeded orange, red and yellow bell pepper, cut in chunks
   Thai Rice Pilaf: recipe follows
   cilantro sprigs
   lime slices

Gently pound chicken to ½-inch thickness. Cut each thigh in half and place in medium glass bowl. In blender container, place soy sauce, brown sugar, catsup, lime juice, shallot and peanut butter. Process on high speed until smooth; pour over chicken, cover and refrigerate at least 15 minutes. Drain chicken. Place marinade in saucepan over medium temperature; cook, stirring occasionally, until slightly thickened, about 6 minutes. Reduce heat, cover and keep warm. Cut onion into 8 wedges; separate each wedge in half. On each of 4 long metal skewers, alternately thread chicken, onion and peppers. Place on broiler pan. Coat kabobs evenly with cooking spray. Broil about 8 inches from heat for about 8 minutes. Turn kabobs, brush liberally with sauce and continue broiling until kabobs begin to glaze. To serve, place skewers on bed of Thai Rice Pilaf. Garnish with cilantro and lime slices. Makes 4 servings.

Thai Rice Pilaf: In medium saucepan, place 2 tablespoons canola oil and heat to medium-high. Add 1 package (7 oz.) curry rice mix. Sauté until rice is lightly toasted. Add 2½ cups low-salt chicken broth and 1 teaspoon spicy seasoned salt. Bring to a boil, cover and reduce heat. Simmer about 25 minutes or until liquid is absorbed. Gently fold in 3 tablespoons chopped cilantro, 2 tablespoons fresh lime juice and ½ teaspoon grated lime peel.

Gloria Pleasants, Virginia

Prize Winners All

Judges at a Cook-Off don't have an easy job. It's often difficult even after five top recipes have been selected to decide the order in which prizes will be awarded. Here are some of the best recipes from past Contests that scored high but didn't quite make first place.

Chili Citrus Chicken

4   boneless, skinless
    chicken breast halves
1½ teaspoons chili powder
½ teaspoon ground cumin
½ teaspoon garlic salt
¼ teaspoon cayenne
    pepper
1   tablespoon vegetable oil

¼ cup fresh lemon juice
¼ cup fresh lime juice
3   tablespoons jalapeno
    pepper jelly
    cilantro sprigs
    red chili peppers
    lemon slices

In small dish, mix together chili powder, cumin, garlic salt and cayenne pepper. Rub mixture on each chicken breast half. In frypan, place oil and heat to medium temperature. Add chicken and cook, turning, about 12 minutes or until chicken is brown and fork can be inserted with ease. Remove chicken to warm platter and keep warm. In frypan, place lemon juice, lime juice and jalapeno pepper jelly; bring to a boil. Cook, stirring constantly, about 1 minute or until mixture thickens. Spoon sauce over chicken. Garnish with cilantro sprigs, red chili pepper and lemon slices. Makes 4 servings.

Mary King, Oklahoma
40th Contest

Chicken Santa Fe

2 whole chicken breasts,
   halved, boned and
   skinned

4 tablespoons jalapeno
   jelly, melted

2 sweet red peppers,
   roasted, skinned*

   Marinade: recipe
   follows

Place chicken between 2 pieces wax paper and gently pound to
1/4-inch thickness. In large resealable plastic bag, place chicken
in single layer. Add marinade, close bag, refrigerate and
marinate, turning once, for 1 hour. Remove chicken from
marinade and place on broiler pan; brush liberally with
marinade. Arrange rack so chicken is 6 inches from heat and
broil about 8 minutes. Turn and broil 8 minutes more or until
chicken is brown and fork can be inserted with ease. Brush
chicken with melted jelly. Place 2 roasted pepper strips to form
an "X" on each breast half; spoon on remaining jelly. Return
chicken to oven and broil until brown and slightly glazed.
Makes 4 servings.

Marinade: In medium bowl, mix together 1/4 cup olive oil, juice
and zest of 1 small lime, 1 clove garlic (crushed), 1 ounce tequila,
1/4 teaspoon bottled hot pepper sauce, 1/8 teaspoon liquid smoke
and 1/4 teaspoon salt.

*To roast peppers, place under broiler, turning often until
 charred. Cool. With point of sharp knife, remove stem, seeds
 and skin. Cut in 8 strips.

June Holley, Ohio
38th Contest

Pesto Stuffed Chicken Legs

8	chicken legs (drumstick-thigh attached)	3	tablespoons butter, divided
¾	cup sliced fresh mushrooms		Mustard Dipping Sauce: recipe follows
1½	cups fresh basil		basil sprigs
2	cloves garlic		cherry tomatoes
1	tablespoon minced fresh ginger		

In blender container, place mushrooms, basil, garlic, ginger and 2 tablespoons of the butter. To make pesto, blend to smooth paste consistency. Starting at thigh end, loosen top skin of chicken to create small pouch over thigh portion of leg. Fill pouch with pesto and pull skin back to original position. (To prevent skin from shrinking when cooking, pierce skin with tip of knife between pouch and leg bone.) In baking pan with roasting rack, place chicken on rack and brush lightly with remaining 1 tablespoon butter, softened. Bake in 450°F. oven about 35 minutes or until brown and fork can be inserted in chicken with ease. Brush lightly with Mustard Dipping Sauce. To serve, line tray with basil sprigs; place chicken legs on top, stuffing side up. Garnish with cherry tomatoes. Pass remaining Mustard Dipping Sauce. Makes 4 servings.

Mustard Dipping Sauce: In small bowl, place 4 teaspoons dry mustard, 6 tablespoons lite soy sauce, 4 tablespoons cider vinegar, 2 teaspoons sesame oil and 1 teaspoon sugar; whisk to combine. Let rest 5 minutes before serving.

Steven Craig, Illinois
39th Contest

Lagoon Chicken Salad

4 boneless, skinless chicken breast halves

1½ cups unsweetened apple juice

3 cups cooked wild rice, prepared according to package instructions

1½ cups seedless green grapes, halved

1 cup chopped unpeeled apple

½ cup chopped celery

¾ cup slivered almonds, divided

½ cup chopped water chestnuts

Dressing: recipe follows

spinach leaves

In deep saucepan, place chicken. Add apple juice and cook over medium heat about 15 minutes or until fork can be inserted in chicken with ease. Remove chicken from pan; reserve broth for other use, if desired. Dice chicken and chill. Gently toss together chicken, wild rice, grapes, apple, celery, ½ cup of the slivered almonds and water chestnuts. Add dressing and toss lightly. Cover and chill about 30 minutes to blend flavors. To serve, place spinach leaves on platter; spoon on chicken mixture and sprinkle with remaining ¼ cup slivered almonds. Makes 4 servings.

Dressing: Mix together 1 cup mayonnaise, ½ teaspoon seasoned salt and ¼ teaspoon cinnamon.

Gloria Kirchman, Minnesota
37th Contest

Basil-Garlic Chicken Pastries

4	boneless, skinless chicken breast halves	½	teaspoon dried basil leaves
½	cup plus 4 tablespoons butter, divided	¼	teaspoon ground ginger
1	carrot, cut in 3-inch strips	¾	teaspoon garlic powder, divided
1	celery stalk, cut in 3-inch strips	4	phyllo pastry sheets
1	small onion, cut in 8 wedges		Basil-Garlic Cream Sauce: recipe follows
½	teaspoon lemon pepper seasoning		parsley sprigs

On half of each chicken breast half, place 1½ teaspoons butter, 1 strip each of carrot and celery and 1 onion wedge. Mix together lemon pepper seasoning, basil leaves, ginger and ¼ teaspoon garlic powder; sprinkle over chicken. Fold other half of chicken over vegetables. Melt ½ cup butter; brush on phyllo sheets and place chicken in center of each at one end. Roll chicken, folding, to opposite end of phyllo sheet; trim excess and seal edges. Place, seam side down, on buttered baking dish; brush with remaining butter. Place in 350°F. oven for 1 hour or until brown. In small frypan, place remaining 1 tablespoon butter and remaining ½ teaspoon garlic powder; add remaining carrot and celery strips and onion wedges. Sauté until tender crisp and set aside. Place chicken on platter; ladle on warm Basil-Garlic Cream Sauce and garnish with sautéed vegetables and parsley. Makes 4 servings.

Basil-Garlic Cream Sauce: Melt ¼ cup butter; add ½ teaspoon dried basil and 1 teaspoon garlic powder. Stir in 2 tablespoons flour; add ½ cup chicken stock, stirring until bubbly. Add 1 cup half-and-half, stirring. Add salt and pepper, if desired.

Gerald Payne, Kentucky
36th Contest

Bittersweet Farm Chicken

1	cut-up chicken	¼	cup lemon juice
½	cup flour	¼	cup orange-flavored liqueur
1	teaspoon salt		
¼	teaspoon pepper	1	tablespoon soy sauce
8	tablespoons butter, divided	¼	cup honey
2	tablespoons julienne orange peel	8	whole cooked baby carrots

In plastic bag, mix together flour, salt and pepper. Add chicken, a few pieces at a time, and shake to coat all sides. In large baking pan, place 4 tablespoons of the butter and heat to melt. Roll chicken in butter to coat all sides and arrange, skin side down, in single layer. Bake in 350°F. oven for 30 minutes. In small saucepan, place remaining 4 tablespoons butter and melt over medium heat. Stir in orange peel, lemon juice, liqueur, soy sauce and honey. Set aside 2 tablespoons mixture. Remove chicken from oven, turn and pour orange-honey mixture over chicken. Return to oven and bake, basting occasionally, 30 minutes longer or until chicken is glazed and fork can be inserted with ease. Add reserved orange-honey mixture to carrots and serve with chicken. Makes 4 servings.

Ann Combs, New Hampshire
37th Contest

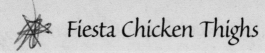

Fiesta Chicken Thighs

8 skinless chicken thighs

⅓ cup flour

1 teaspoon garlic salt

1 teaspoon lemon pepper

1 teaspoon chili powder

2 tablespoons margarine

2 tablespoons olive oil

¼ cup hot jalapeno jelly

2 large limes; 1½ sliced, ½ reserved

2 teaspoons chopped parsley

lemon slices

ripe olives

parsley sprigs

red cherry peppers

In plastic bag, mix together flour, garlic salt, lemon pepper and chili powder. Add chicken and shake to coat. In large frypan, place margarine and olive oil; heat over medium temperature. Add chicken and cook, turning, about 10 minutes or until brown on all sides. Reduce heat, cover and cook 5 minutes. Remove cover and cook about 5 minutes more or until fork can be inserted in chicken with ease. Remove chicken from frypan. Turn chicken crosswise, meaty side up, and cut diagonally into chicken 3 or 4 times. On foil-lined pan, place chicken and spoon jalapeno jelly evenly over chicken, spreading with fork. Bake in 400°F. oven about 5 minutes or until jelly melts. Squeeze juice from reserved ½ lime over chicken. Remove chicken to serving dish and sprinkle with chopped parsley. Garnish with lemon slices, olives, parsley sprigs and red cherry peppers. Makes 4 servings.

Beverly Sebastian, Texas
39th Contest

Chefs Cook Chicken

Chicken is the favorite meat of creative chefs. A tasty protein which is compatible with most fruits and vegetables, chicken adapts well to a seemingly endless variety of seasonings. These chicken recipes are served in leading restaurants across the nation.

Sautéed Chicken Breast with Melon Sauce

(Pictured in color section)

4 whole boneless, skinless chicken breasts

¼ honeydew melon

¼ cantaloupe

2 tablespoons vegetable oil

1 teaspoon salt

½ teaspoon pepper

¾ cup sake or Riesling wine

¼ cup chicken broth

1 teaspoon freshly grated ginger

2 teaspoons cornstarch

¼ cup rice wine vinegar

1 tablespoon honey

1 tablespoon butter

1 tablespoon chopped parsley

Cut each chicken breast in half and slightly flatten with palm of hand. Peel melons and slice into thin strips (or cut into melon balls). Place vegetable oil in large frypan over medium heat. Sprinkle chicken with salt and pepper and add to pan; sauté about 5 minutes on each side until golden brown. Add sake (or wine), chicken broth and ginger; simmer for several minutes. Dissolve cornstarch in rice wine vinegar. Remove chicken to serving platter. To frypan, add vinegar mixture, honey and melons, stirring gently. Add butter and parsley; dribble sauce over chicken. Makes 8 servings.

Chef Kaspar Donier, Kaspar's
Seattle

Tangy Chicken with Shiitake Crust

6	large boneless, skinless chicken breasts	2	large cloves garlic, minced
2	tablespoons olive oil	1	teaspoon salt
¾	pound button mushrooms, ends trimmed, sliced	½	teaspoon freshly ground pepper
¾	pound shiitake mushrooms, ends trimmed, sliced	2	tablespoons minced fresh chervil, thyme or chives
2	large shallots, peeled, coarsely chopped	¼	stick chilled butter, coarsely chopped
			Tangy Sauce: recipe follows

In large frypan, place oil over medium-high heat. Add mushrooms, shallots and garlic; cook, stirring, until lightly browned, about 5 minutes. Cool; add salt and pepper. Remove small fillets from underside of chicken breasts and place fillets in food processor; grind to smooth paste, pulsing on/off. Add mushroom mixture and chop coarsely. Line large baking sheet with parchment. Gently pound chicken breasts to even thickness. Divide mushroom mixture into 6 parts (about ½ cup each). On 12-inch sheet of plastic wrap, place 1 part mushroom mixture in center. Fold plastic over mixture; pat to even thickness slightly larger than 1 chicken breast. Place chicken on top of mixture, smooth side down. Gather plastic up around chicken until mixture adheres to top and sides of chicken. Unwrap and invert chicken, uncoated side down, onto baking sheet. Repeat with remaining chicken, place in 350°F. oven and bake about 12 minutes. Remove from oven; let rest 12 minutes. Slice chicken diagonally; arrange on serving plate, fanning slices. Reheat Tangy Sauce; stir in chervil and butter. Ladle sauce beside chicken. Makes 6 servings.

Tangy Sauce: Remove orange part of peel from 2 oranges; chop peel coarsely and place in saucepan with 2 shallots (peeled and coarsely chopped). Add 1 cup dry white wine and 1 cup balsamic vinegar; boil over medium-high heat until reduced to ½ cup. Add 2 cups unsalted chicken stock; whisk in 2 tablespoons tomato paste; boil to reduce to 1 cup. Strain, pressing on ingredients.

Chef Michel Richard, Citrus Restaurant, Los Angeles

Grilled Chicken with Corn-Tomato Salsa

6	chicken breast halves	3	sprigs thyme
½	cup olive oil	2	tablespoons Dijon mustard
1	teaspoon cracked black pepper		
2	cloves garlic, minced		Corn-Tomato Salsa: recipe follows
2	sprigs rosemary		

In small saucepan, place olive oil, pepper, garlic, rosemary and thyme. Over low heat, bring to a very warm stage (do not boil). Remove from heat and cool. Brush mustard over chicken, pour marinade over chicken, cover and marinate in refrigerator overnight. Remove chicken from marinade and shake off any excess. Place on prepared grill, skin side down, about 6 inches from heat. Grill over medium heat about 12 minutes, turning once. (Note: chicken can be broiled if grill is not available.) To serve, place chicken on plate and top with Corn-Tomato Salsa. Makes 6 servings.

Corn-Tomato Salsa: In food processor, coarsely chop 6 Roma tomatoes which have been cored and seeded. Stir in 1¼ cups cooked fresh corn kernels, 2 tablespoons chopped jalapeno chile, 1 finely diced small red onion, 2 tablespoons cider vinegar and 1 tablespoon diced basil. Let stand about 1 hour to blend flavors.

Chef Patrick Clark, Tavern on the Green New York

Baked Chicken Breast with Cornbread-Collard Stuffing

8	whole boneless, skinless chicken breasts	1	egg, slightly beaten
1	stick butter, divided	1	teaspoon ground sage
1	small sweet onion, diced	½	teaspoon salt
3	cups collard greens, washed, chopped	¼	teaspoon pepper
2	cups crumbled cornbread		Sweet Onion Gravy: recipe follows
			cooked rice

In large frypan, place all but 1 tablespoon butter; melt over medium heat. Add onion and sauté until transparent. Add collard greens and cook until tender, about 3 minutes. Remove from heat and place in large bowl. Add cornbread, egg and sage; mix well and cool. Gently pound chicken breasts until slightly flattened. Place ⅛ of stuffing on center of each; roll and tuck ends under. In large, greased baking pan, place chicken. Brush with remaining tablespoon butter; sprinkle with salt and pepper. Place in 375°F. oven and cook about 20 minutes or until fork can be inserted in chicken with ease. Slice each breast into 5 slices and arrange on plate with Sweet Onion Gravy and rice. Makes 8 servings.

Sweet Onion Gravy: In frypan, place 4 tablespoons butter; melt over medium heat. Add 2 thinly-sliced sweet onions and sauté until transparent. Add 2 cups chicken broth, ½ cup heavy cream, ½ teaspoon brown food coloring, ½ teaspoon salt and ¼ teaspoon pepper; bring to a boil. In ¼ cup cold water, dissolve 2 tablespoons cornstarch; add some gravy from frypan and stir to mix well. Add cornstarch mixture to gravy, stirring to prevent lumps. Bring to a boil, stirring, until thickened.

Chef Steve Kish, 82 Queen Restaurant
Charleston, SC

Molasses and Honey Marinated Chicken Breast

4	large boneless, skinless chicken breast halves	2	tablespoons molasses
½	teaspoon salt	2	tablespoons honey
⅛	teaspoon freshly ground pepper	1	lime, juiced
¾	cup whiskey	2	tablespoons olive oil
2	tablespoons grain mustard	1	cup chicken stock
		¼	cup butter

Sprinkle chicken with salt and pepper. In small saucepan, place whiskey; boil over medium heat about 5 minutes, reducing liquid by half (all alcohol will evaporate). Remove from heat and add mustard, molasses, honey and lime juice. Stir to mix well; remove half of mixture and reserve. In remaining half, place chicken and marinate in refrigerator at least 1 hour or overnight. In large frypan, place oil over medium heat. Add chicken and cook, turning once, about 10 minutes or until fork can be inserted with ease. Remove chicken from frypan and keep warm. To frypan, add chicken stock and cook to reduce by two-thirds. Add reserved marinade and butter; simmer, stirring, until butter melts. Pour over chicken. Makes 4 servings.

Chef Sarah Stegner, Ritz-Carlton Chicago

Cumin Crusted Chicken with Borracho Beans and Greens

(Pictured in color section)

4 chicken breast quarters	2 tablespoons olive oil
Toasted Cumin and Black Pepper Rub: recipe follows	2 tablespoons butter
	2 shallots, minced
Borracho Beans: recipe follows	1 pound mustard greens, washed, stemmed

Rub chicken with Toasted Cumin and Black Pepper Rub. Refrigerate at least 2 hours. Prepare Borracho Beans and keep hot. In frypan over medium heat, place oil. Add chicken and sear on each side. Remove chicken to 350°F. oven and cook about 45 minutes or until fork can be inserted with ease. In large frypan, place butter and shallots; cook, stirring, about 2 minutes. Add mustard greens and cook, tossing gently, until wilted. Arrange greens in 4 shallow bowls. Add beans evenly around greens and top with chicken. Makes 4 servings.

Toasted Cumin and Black Pepper Rub: In frypan, place ¼ cup cumin seeds, 2 tablespoons dried oregano, 1 tablespoon black peppercorns, ¼ teaspoon salt and ½ teaspoon sugar. Toast over medium heat, stirring, about 2 minutes. Transfer to spice grinder and pulse until smooth.

Borracho Beans: Wash 1 cup dried pinto beans; cover with water and soak overnight. Drain and rinse beans; place in saucepan and add water to cover by 3 inches. Simmer over low heat about 1½ hours until tender, adding water if necessary. Drain. In large frypan over medium heat, place 1 tablespoon vegetable oil, ¼ onion (diced) and 6 serrano chiles with seeds (minced). Cook about 5 minutes; stir in 8 plum tomatoes (diced), ⅔ cup beer and ¼ teaspoon salt. Add beans, bring to a boil, reduce heat and simmer about 10 minutes. Stir in 2 tablespoons chopped fresh cilantro leaves just before serving.

Chef Mark Kiffin, Coyote Cafe
Santa Fe

Capital Chicken Salad

4 boneless, skinless chicken breast halves

Marinade: recipe follows

1 cup garbanzo beans, drained

4 tablespoons chopped green chilies

2 avocados, peeled, diced

2 medium tomatoes, cored, seeded, diced

1 head Romaine lettuce, cut in thin strips

½ cup Spicy Lime Dressing: recipe follows

28 blue corn tortilla chips

4 teaspoons sour cream

4 tablespoons bottled tomato salsa

Place chicken in Marinade and refrigerate about 4 hours. On prepared grill, cook chicken about 10 minutes, turning once, or sauté in heavy frypan sprayed with vegetable spray. In large bowl, mix together garbanzo beans, chilies, avocados, tomatoes, lettuce and Spicy Lime Dressing; gently toss. On individual plates or bowls, arrange 6 tortilla chips around edge with portion of salad mixture in center. Cut each chicken breast half into 4 or 5 strips and place on top with 1 tortilla chip in center topped with 1 teaspoon sour cream and 1 tablespoon salsa. Makes 4 servings.

Marinade: In blender, place 1½ cups fresh pineapple juice, 3 tablespoons honey, 2 tablespoons sesame oil, ½ cup cider vinegar, 2 tablespoons sugar, 4 cloves garlic, 4 tablespoons ground chili, ½ teaspoon ground coriander and ½ teaspoon ground cumin. Blend until smooth.

Spicy Lime Dressing: In blender, place ¼ clove garlic, ½ shallot, ½ teaspoon ground chili, 1½ tablespoons red wine vinegar, 2 tablespoons fresh lime juice, ¾ teaspoon Dijon mustard, ¾ teaspoon puréed ancho chili, ¼ teaspoon salt and ⅛ teaspoon pepper. Process on medium speed, slowly adding ½ cup peanut oil.

Chefs Jeffrey and Sallie Buben, Vidalia Washington, DC

Slow Cooked Chicken with Asiago Creamy Grits

(Pictured in color section)

6	chicken legs, cut into leg and thigh	4	bay leaves
3	tablespoons butter, divided	1	pound wild mushrooms (morels, porcinis, criminis or shiitakes)
6	carrots	1	tablespoon dried porcini, soaked in warm water
4	stalks celery		
3	onions	3	cups chicken stock
2	leeks		Asiago Creamy Grits: recipe follows
6	shallots		
1	bunch thyme		

In large cast iron skillet, place 2 tablespoons butter over medium heat. Add chicken and sear until golden brown; remove to rack while cooking vegetables. Drain off excess oil, add remaining tablespoon butter, carrots, celery, onions, leeks, shallots, thyme and bay leaves. Sauté over medium heat about 10 minutes. Add dried mushrooms, then chicken stock and chicken; bring to a boil. Cover with foil and place in 300°F. oven for 1½ hours. (While chicken is cooking, prepare grits.) Lift out chicken and strain liquid. Skim sauce, reduce by ¼ and reserve. In large individual bowl, place 1 large scoop grits; top with chicken leg and thigh. Ladle on reserved mushroom broth and sautéed mushrooms. Garnish with fresh herbs and grated Asiago cheese. Makes 6 servings.

Asiago Creamy Grits: In large saucepan, place 2 cups water, 1 cup chicken stock, 1 tablespoon chopped garlic, ¼ teaspoon salt and ⅛ teaspoon pepper. Bring to a boil and whisk in 1 cup stone ground grits. Cook on low 15 minutes, stirring frequently. Remove from heat and add 1 cup heavy cream and 1 cup grated Asiago cheese. Cover until ready to serve.

Chef Frank Stitt, Highlands Bar & Grill
Birmingham, AL

Cajun Chicken and Dumplings

1	large chicken	2	hard-cooked eggs, chopped
2	quarts salted water		
¼	cup butter	1	tablespoon Worcestershire sauce
½	cup sliced mushrooms		
½	cup chopped celery	1	teaspoon vinegar
½	cup chopped green bell pepper	½	teaspoon cayenne pepper
1	pimento, chopped	⅛	teaspoon white pepper
¼	cup chopped onion	⅛	teaspoon black pepper
1	quart milk		Dumplings: recipe follows

In large saucepan, place chicken and water over medium heat. Simmer about 45 minutes or until fork tender. Remove chicken; reserve broth. Chop chicken in large pieces, discarding skin and bones; set aside. In medium frypan, place butter over low heat. Add mushrooms, celery, bell pepper, pimento and onion; sauté about 2 minutes. To broth in saucepan, add milk, eggs, Worcestershire sauce, vinegar, cayenne, white and black peppers. Stir in sautéed vegetables; heat to boil, reduce heat to simmer and add alternating layers of chicken and dumplings, pushing each layer down into broth. Simmer about 15 minutes or until dumplings are tender. Serve chicken, dumplings and broth in individual bowls. Makes 6 servings.

Dumplings: In medium bowl, place 2 cups flour, 1 teaspoon each salt, garlic salt, ground white and black peppers. Add ¼ teaspoon each cayenne pepper, garlic powder, thyme and oregano; also, 1 teaspoon baking powder. Stir in 1 slightly beaten egg, ½ stick softened butter and 1 teaspoon olive oil. Gradually stir in ½ cup milk. Knead dough until soft and smooth; divide into 5 small balls. Roll each ball on floured board until paper thin; cut into strips 1½ inches wide and 3 inches long. Lay strips on wax paper about 15 minutes before adding to broth.

Chef T. J. Robinson, Gingerbread House
Oakland, CA

Chicken Salads

Chicken salads are easy to prepare, nutritious and offer great versatility in combining ingredients. Light or hearty, chicken salad can be an entrée, a side dish or even an appetizer for lunch or dinner, as well as party fare. These recipes are tasty examples of why chicken salad has become a popular year-round menu item.

Barbecued Thai Chicken Salad

1	whole broiler-fryer chicken	2	tablespoons brown sugar
1	can (14 oz.) unsweetened coconut milk	12	red lettuce leaves
1	tablespoon curry powder	1	medium head lettuce, shredded
1	tablespoon lime juice	1	large red bell pepper, cut in strips
1	tablespoon fish sauce	½	cup torn mint leaves
3	cloves garlic, minced		Sweet and Sour Cilantro Dressing: recipe follows
¼	cup chopped cilantro leaves	⅓	cup finely chopped peanuts

Cut chicken in half with sharp knife. In large bowl, place coconut milk and whisk in curry powder. Add lime juice, fish sauce, garlic, cilantro and sugar; mix well. Add chicken, turning to coat. Cover and refrigerate at least 4 hours or overnight. On prepared grill (or in oven broiler), place chicken, skin side down. Cook about 10 minutes, turn and continue cooking until fork can be inserted in chicken with ease, about 30 minutes. Cool chicken slightly and cut into strips. On 6 individual plates, arrange red lettuce leaves. Mix together shredded lettuce, bell pepper and mint; portion equally onto red lettuce. Place chicken strips on top. Sprinkle with peanuts and serve with Sweet and Sour Cilantro Dressing. Makes 6 servings.

Sweet and Sour Cilantro Dressing: In medium bowl, mix together ⅔ cup rice vinegar, ¼ cup sugar, ¼ cup minced cilantro, ¼ teaspoon salt, ½ teaspoon chili paste and ⅓ cup safflower oil. Stir until sugar dissolves.

Chicken Salad with Goat Cheese

4   chicken breast halves, boned, with skin
6   cups mixed salad greens
½   small red onion, thinly sliced
1   carrot, cut in strips
1   yellow bell pepper, cut in strips
5   ounces goat cheese, cut in 4 pieces

4   sprigs rosemary
1   tablespoon olive oil
½   teaspoon salt
⅛   teaspoon pepper
   Salad Vinaigrette: recipe follows
¼   cup pine nuts, toasted

In large bowl, place salad greens, onion, carrot and bell pepper; chill. Under skin of each chicken breast half, insert 1 piece of goat cheese and 1 sprig of rosemary. Pull skin back over meat, brush chicken with oil and sprinkle with salt and pepper. Place chicken on broiler pan, skin side up. Broil about 7 minutes, turn and cook about 7 minutes longer or until fork can be inserted in chicken with ease. To chilled vegetables, add Salad Vinaigrette and toss; divide evenly on 4 plates. Place chicken on cutting board and slice. Arrange chicken slices on salad and sprinkle with pine nuts. Makes 4 servings.

Salad Vinaigrette: Whisk together ⅓ cup olive oil, 2 tablespoons balsamic vinegar, 1 minced garlic clove, ½ teaspoon salt and ¼ teaspoon pepper.

Fennel and Walnut Chicken Salad

6 large chicken thighs, skinned	1 teaspoon chives
1 stalk fennel	3 tablespoons chopped toasted walnuts
4 tablespoons mayonnaise	

Cut off tall stalk and feathery leaves from fennel bulb; rinse well and cut in half. Reserve 2 tablespoons minced fennel leaves. Trim base from fennel bulb and remove tough outer layers. Slice fennel hearts crosswise into $\frac{1}{2}$-inch pieces; measure $\frac{1}{2}$ cup and set aside. In large saucepan, place chicken, fennel stalk and remaining leaves. Add water to cover and bring to a boil over high heat. Reduce heat to low and simmer about 25 minutes or until fork can be inserted in chicken with ease. Remove chicken from broth and cut into chunks when cool enough to handle. In medium bowl, mix together mayonnaise, reserved minced fennel leaves and chives. Add chicken, sliced fennel and walnuts, tossing to mix well. Makes 4 servings.

Chicken Satay Salad

2¼ pounds boneless, skinless chicken breast, cut in strips

24 bamboo skewers

2 cups Thai peanut sauce, divided

¼ cup chopped roasted peanuts

1 pound mixed salad greens, chopped

¾ cup sesame-with-soy salad dressing

1 papaya, peeled, seeded and sliced

1 avocado, peeled, seeded and sliced

1 large cucumber, seeded and diced

1 large red bell pepper, julienne cut

3 ounces enoki mushrooms

Thread about 1½ ounces of the chicken breast strips onto each bamboo skewer; place on sheet tray. With 1 cup of the Thai peanut sauce, mix the chopped peanuts; pour over chicken. Marinate in refrigerator at least 1 hour. Arrange skewers on lightly oiled broiler pan and broil (or grill) about 2 minutes per side, basting with remaining 1 cup Thai peanut sauce. Toss mixed salad greens with sesame-with-soy salad dressing and arrange on 6 individual plates. Place 4 chicken skewers in criss-cross fashion on top of greens. Between spokes of skewers, arrange slices of papaya, avocado, cucumber and bell pepper strips. Place sprig of enoki mushrooms in center of salad. Makes 6 servings.

Green Bean Chicken Salad

5   boneless, skinless
    chicken breasts

1   red bell pepper, cut in
    ¼-inch strips

1   green bell pepper, cut
    in ¼-inch strips

1   small red onion, sliced

½   pound fresh green
    beans, snapped and
    blanched

    Dressing: recipe
    follows

Place chicken on prepared grill and cook about 5 minutes per side. Chill in refrigerator; cut into ¼-inch strips. In large mixing bowl, place chicken, red and green pepper, onion and green beans. Add dressing and toss gently to mix well. Serve with chilled fresh fruits, if desired. Makes 8 servings.

Dressing: In medium bowl, mix together 1 cup mayonnaise, 1 jar (6 oz.) Creole mustard, 1 teaspoon cider vinegar, 1 teaspoon sugar, ½ teaspoon salt and ¼ teaspoon white pepper.

South-of-the-Border Chicken Salad

4½ cups cooked, diced chicken

2¾ cups whole kernel corn, well drained

2½ cups canned black beans, drained

1 cup diced red pepper

1 cup diced green pepper

1½ cups thinly sliced scallions

2 tablespoons thinly sliced, seeded jalapeno pepper

⅔ cup pine nuts, toasted

½ cup prepared hickory flavor barbecue sauce

¾ cup prepared Italian salad dressing (not creamy)

2 tablespoons chili powder

1 tablespoon cumin

2½ tablespoons fresh lime juice

2½ tablespoons chopped cilantro

1½ teaspoons hot pepper sauce

In large bowl, mix together chicken, corn, black beans, red and green pepper, scallions, jalapeno pepper and pine nuts; toss gently to mix well. In another bowl, mix together barbecue sauce, Italian dressing, chili powder, cumin, lime juice, cilantro and hot pepper sauce; stir to mix well. Pour dressing mixture over chicken mixture and toss to coat evenly. Refrigerate, covered, 3 hours or overnight. Serve in a large, fried tortilla shell over a bed of shredded lettuce. If desired, garnish with dollops of sour cream, chopped black olives and shredded cheddar cheese. Makes 6 serving.

Chunky Chicken and Cucumber Salad

1   whole chicken, cooked, skinned, boned, cut into chunks

2   cucumbers, peeled, cubed

1   sweet red pepper, chopped

1   tablespoon apple cider vinegar

½   teaspoon salt

¼   teaspoon pepper

¼   teaspoon seasoned salt

4   ounces plain nonfat yogurt

    endive

In medium bowl, mix together cucumber and pepper; sprinkle with vinegar, salt and pepper. Let sit about 5 minutes. Stir in chicken, seasoned salt and yogurt, tossing gently. Cover and refrigerate until completely chilled. Serve on dark curly endive. Makes 4 servings.

Fat-Conscious Dishes

Limiting fat intake is important to healthful eating. Chicken is naturally low in fat content — especially in saturated fat. Chicken is also naturally pleasing to the palate. It's easy to retain nutritional benefits without losing taste appeal with recipes that keep a watchful eye on total fat content.

Mint and Ginger Chicken

1½ pounds boneless, skinless chicken breast, cut in ½-inch cubes

2 tablespoons flour

2 tablespoons fish sauce

2 tablespoons dark soy sauce, divided

1½ inch piece ginger, peeled

2 green chilies, chopped

1 tablespoon vinegar

1 tablespoon sugar

1 lime, peel grated and juice divided

3 cups chopped napa cabbage

4 green onions, chopped

¼ cup chopped fresh mint

In medium bowl, place chicken. Sprinkle with flour, turning to coat. Add fish sauce and 1 tablespoon of the soy sauce; set aside. Place ginger in blender or food processor and mince, about 30 seconds; add chilies, remaining 1 tablespoon soy sauce, vinegar, sugar and ½ teaspoon grated lime peel. Blend or process about 1 minute; set aside. Spray wok or Dutch oven with nonstick cooking spray and heat to high temperature. Add chicken, onion and cabbage, stir-frying about 4 minutes until chicken turns white. Pour ginger sauce mixture over chicken and continue to stir-fry until sauce thickens, about 2 minutes. Sprinkle with lime juice and top with mint. Serve hot with rice, if desired. Makes 4 servings.

Total fat per serving: 2.5 grams

Deluxe Microwave
Chicken Breasts

4   whole boneless, skinless chicken breasts, halved

3   tablespoons bottled microwave browning sauce

1   teaspoon seasoned salt, divided

½   teaspoon coarsely ground pepper, divided

1   cup nonfat plain yogurt

1   teaspoon grated onion

1   teaspoon prepared mustard

Brush chicken with browning sauce and arrange on rack around outside edges of circular microwave dish. Cover loosely with wax paper and microwave on HIGH for 6 minutes. Remove chicken from rack and place in bottom of dish, turning breasts over and keeping them in a circle around edge of dish. Sprinkle with ½ teaspoon of the salt and ¼ teaspoon of the pepper. In small bowl, mix together yogurt, onion and mustard; spoon over chicken, dividing equally on each piece. Cover loosely with wax paper and microwave on HIGH 6 minutes or until fork can be inserted in chicken with ease. Sprinkle with remaining ½ teaspoon salt and ¼ teaspoon pepper. Let stand 2 minutes, then remove chicken to warm serving platter. Stir pan juices to mix well and pour into bowl to pass and spoon over rice or pasta, if served with chicken. Makes 8 servings.

Total fat per serving: 1.5 grams

Grilled Caribbean
Chicken Breasts

4	boneless, skinless chicken breast halves	1	teaspoon grated ginger-root
¼	cup fresh orange juice	1	clove garlic, minced
1	teaspoon grated orange peel	¼	teaspoon hot pepper sauce
1	tablespoon olive oil	½	teaspoon oregano
1	tablespoon fresh lime juice	½	teaspoon salt
		¼	teaspoon pepper

In large shallow bowl, mix together orange juice, orange peel, olive oil, lime juice, ginger, garlic, hot pepper sauce and oregano. Add chicken, turning to coat. Cover and marinate in refrigerator about 3 hours or overnight. Remove chicken from marinade and sprinkle with salt and pepper. Place on prepared grill about 6 inches from heat. (Chicken may also be broiled, if desired.) Grill, turning, about 10 minutes or until fork can be inserted in chicken with ease. Makes 4 servings.

Total fat per serving: 6.0 grams.

Layered Chicken Salad

1 whole chicken, cooked, boned, skinned, broken into pieces

1 can (8 oz.) water chestnuts, drained, sliced

2 cups alfalfa sprouts

1 small red onion, thinly sliced, broken into rings

½ cup fat-free Italian dressing

½ teaspoon freshly ground pepper

In medium glass bowl, layer half of each of the following ingredients in this order: chicken, water chestnuts, alfalfa sprouts and onion rings. Sprinkle with half of the dressing and half of the pepper. Repeat layers and sprinkle with remaining dressing and pepper. Cover and refrigerate at least 2 hours. Serve cold. Makes 4 servings.

Total fat per serving: 7.0 grams

Cajun Chicken Breasts

4	boneless, skinless chicken breast halves	¼	teaspoon salt
2	cloves garlic, minced	¼	teaspoon cayenne pepper
1	tablespoon fresh, finely chopped parsley	¼	teaspoon dried mint
		2	tablespoons white wine

In shallow refrigerator dish with cover, mix together garlic, parsley, salt, cayenne pepper and mint; stir in wine. Spread mixture on all sides of chicken breasts, cover and refrigerate at least 3 hours or overnight. Spray nonstick frypan with cooking spray and heat over medium-high temperature. Add chicken and cook about 5 minutes; turn chicken and cook about 5 minutes more or until fork can be inserted with ease. Makes 4 servings.

Total fat per serving: 3.0 grams

Grilled Chicken

Cooking on the grill is popular all across America, and no food is better cooked on the grill than chicken. Whether a backyard charcoal grill or an elaborate gas or electric grill is used, chicken can be prepared in many tempting ways. Or, if it's more convenient, chicken in the following recipes can be broiled.

Spicy Grilled Chicken Thighs with Black-Eyed Pea and Mango Salsa

(Pictured on cover)

8 boneless, skinless chicken thighs

1 tablespoon olive oil

1½ tablespoons fresh lime juice

½ teaspoon ground cumin

3 drops bottled hot pepper sauce

½ teaspoon salt

¼ teaspoon coarsely ground pepper

Black-Eyed Pea and Mango Salsa: recipe follows

cilantro leaves

In shallow pan, whisk together olive oil, lime juice, cumin and hot pepper sauce. Add chicken and turn to coat; sprinkle with salt and pepper. Cover and refrigerate at least 30 minutes or for several hours. Remove chicken from marinade and place on prepared grill about 6 inches from heat. Grill about 4 minutes on each side or until fork can be inserted in chicken with ease. Serve with Black-Eyed Pea and Mango Salsa. Makes 4 servings.

Black-Eyed Pea and Mango Salsa: In large bowl, mix together 16 red cherry tomatoes, quartered; 6 oil-packed sun-dried tomato halves, cut in thin strips; ½ cup cooked black-eyed peas, rinsed and drained; ½ ripe mango, peeled and diced in small cubes; ¼ cup minced red onion; 2 tablespoons fresh lime juice; 2 tablespoons red wine vinegar; 2 tablespoons olive oil; 3 tablespoons minced fresh cilantro; ½ teaspoon salt and ¼ teaspoon freshly ground pepper. Stir gently to mix well and let sit at room temperature 1 hour to allow flavors to blend.

Honey Mustard Grilled Chicken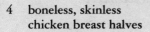

4	boneless, skinless chicken breast halves	2	tablespoons fresh lemon juice
¼	cup honey mustard salad dressing	1	tablespoon honey
3	tablespoons grainy Dijon mustard	½	teaspoon salt
		¼	teaspoon freshly ground pepper

In large bowl, whisk together salad dressing, mustard, lemon juice, honey, salt and pepper. Add chicken and turn to coat well; cover and marinate in refrigerator 1 hour or overnight. Remove chicken from marinade and place on prepared charcoal grill about 6 inches from heat. Grill chicken, turning occasionally, about 35 minutes or until fork can be inserted with ease. Makes 4 servings

Grilled Chicken with Blueberry Chutney

6	boneless chicken breast halves, skin on	2	tablespoons brown sugar
¾	cup fresh orange juice; rind grated and reserved	1½	teaspoons Worcestershire sauce
2	tablespoons red wine vinegar	1	teaspoon Dijon mustard
2	cloves garlic, finely minced	1	orange, sliced for garnish
			Blueberry Chutney: recipe follows

In shallow dish, whisk together orange juice, vinegar, garlic, brown sugar, Worcestershire sauce and Dijon mustard. Reserve ¼ cup plus 3 tablespoons of the mixture. To remaining portion, add chicken, turning to coat. Cover and refrigerate at least 1 hour. Remove chicken from marinade and place on prepared grill about 6 inches from heat. Cook about 6 minutes on each side or until fork can be inserted in chicken with ease, basting once near end of cooking time with reserved 3 tablespoons of the marinade. Serve with Blueberry Chutney; garnish with orange slices. Makes 6 servings.

Blueberry Chutney: In medium saucepan, place 1 tablespoon olive oil and heat over medium heat. Add ⅓ cup finely chopped red onion and sauté until soft, about 2 minutes. Add ½ cup catsup, remaining ¼ cup reserved marinade, 2 cups fresh blueberries, 1 tablespoon fresh lemon juice, 1 tablespoon brown sugar, reserved grated rind of 1 orange and ⅛ teaspoon salt. Simmer on low heat, stirring, about 15 minutes or until mixture thickens slightly. Serve warm.

Peruvian Grilled Chicken Thighs

8   chicken thighs

1   teaspoon ground coriander

¼   teaspoon cayenne pepper

½   teaspoon salt

2   cups rice, cooked according to package directions

Tomato-Cilantro Sauce: recipe follows

1   ripe avocado, peeled, sliced

4   tablespoons sour cream

In small bowl, mix together coriander, cayenne and salt; rub thighs with mixture. On prepared grill, place chicken and cook, turning, about 12 minutes or until internal temperature of 160°F. is reached when tested with a thermometer. Spoon rice onto 4 individual plates, top with Tomato-Cilantro Sauce and arrange chicken on top. Garnish with avocado slices and dollops of sour cream. Makes 4 servings.

Tomato-Cilantro Sauce: In blender or food processor, place 2 coarsely chopped ripe tomatoes, 1 coarsely chopped red onion, 1 coarsely chopped clove garlic, 1 jar (7 oz.) roasted red peppers (drained), ¼ cup cilantro leaves, ¼ teaspoon salt and ⅛ teaspoon pepper; process until smooth.

Rotisserie Chicken with Fresh Tarragon

1	large broiler-fryer chicken	2	tablespoons unsalted butter
4	sprigs fresh tarragon, divided	1	clove garlic, crushed
3	tablespoons olive oil	1	teaspoon salt
		½	teaspoon pepper

Loosen skin of chicken by running fingers between skin and breast meat; insert 1 large sprig tarragon between skin and meat on each breast half. In small frypan, place olive oil, butter and garlic; mince remaining tarragon and add to pan. Place over low heat until mixture sizzles; remove from heat. Sprinkle chicken with salt and pepper. Truss chicken and tie legs together. Thread chicken on rotisserie spit and brush with oil-herb mixture. Cook about 1½ hours or until drumsticks move easily in their sockets and juices from chicken run clear. Baste several times during cooking. When done, a meat thermometer inserted into the thigh will register 180°F. Remove chicken from rotisserie and place on rack to stand for 10 minutes before carving. Remove and discard strings. Garnish with additional fresh herbs.* Makes 4 servings.

*Instead of tarragon, other fresh herbs such as dill, basil, oregano or rosemary may be used.

Any-Day Chicken

Chicken is a convenience food, readily available in a variety of time-saving forms. And it can be quickly and easily prepared in simple ways that the whole family enjoys. These busy-day chicken dishes are so tasty there won't be any hesitation in inviting guests to share the meal.

Easy Chicken Stroganoff

4 boneless, skinless chicken breast halves	1½ cups chicken broth
2 tablespoons butter	2 tablespoons prepared coarse grain mustard
2 tablespoons flour	½ cup sour cream
1 medium red onion, chopped	3 tablespoons chopped parsley
8 ounces mushrooms, quartered	2 cups cooked egg noodles

In large nonstick frypan, place butter and melt over high heat. In shallow dish, place flour; add chicken and turn to coat well. Place chicken in frypan and cook, turning, about 5 minutes to brown on both sides. Stir in onion, mushrooms and any unused flour. Reduce heat to medium and cook, stirring, about 5 minutes or until onion is golden brown. In small bowl, whisk together chicken broth and mustard; pour mixture into frypan and stir. Bring to a boil, reduce heat to simmer and cook about 5 minutes more or until fork can be inserted in chicken with ease. Stir in sour cream and parsley; simmer an additional 2 minutes. Serve over egg noodles. Makes 4 servings.

Quick Chicken and Artichoke Casserole

4   boneless, skinless chicken breast halves

1   can (8 oz.) sliced water chestnuts, drained

1   can (2 oz.) pimento, diced

1   can (13¾ oz.) artichoke hearts, drained, quartered

⅓   cup minced onion

1   cup mayonnaise

¼   teaspoon pepper

½   cup grated Parmesan cheese

⅓   cup dry seasoned bread crumbs

In medium saucepan, place chicken and cover with cold water. Place over high heat and bring to a boil. Reduce heat to low, cover and simmer about 7 minutes. Turn off heat, remove cover and let chicken cool in water for 10 minutes. In large bowl, place water chestnuts, pimento, artichoke hearts, onion, mayonnaise and pepper; stir gently to mix well. In small bowl, stir together Parmesan cheese and bread crumbs. Stir half of crumb mixture into artichoke mixture. Chop chicken and stir into artichoke mixture; spoon into 1½ quart casserole and sprinkle with remaining bread crumbs. Place in 400°F. oven and bake about 35 minutes, until brown and heated through. Makes 4 servings.

Hearty Moroccan Chicken

4   chicken leg quarters, skinned

1   tablespoon olive oil

1   medium onion, cut in chunks

4   cloves garlic, minced

1   tablespoon minced ginger

2   carrots, cut in chunks

1   cup canned chickpeas, drained

$\frac{1}{2}$ cup golden raisins

2   sticks cinnamon

$1\frac{1}{2}$ teaspoons cumin

$\frac{1}{2}$ teaspoon turmeric

5   cups water

2   zucchini, cut in chunks

2   cups prepared couscous

In heavy large nonstick saucepan or Dutch oven, place olive oil over high heat. Add chicken and cook about 10 minutes, turning to brown on all sides. Stir in onion, garlic, ginger, carrots, chickpeas, raisins, cinnamon, cumin, turmeric and water. Bring to a simmer, reduce heat and cook about 20 minutes. Stir in zucchini and simmer an additional 10 minutes. Remove cinnamon sticks. Serve in large bowls over couscous. Makes 4 servings.

Chunky Chili Chicken

1½ pounds boneless, skinless chicken thighs, cut in chunks

5 tablespoons olive oil, divided

1 medium sweet onion, chopped

1 large red bell pepper, diced

3 cloves garlic, minced

1½ teaspoons cumin seed

1 tablespoon chili powder

1 teaspoon dried oregano

1 can (10 oz.) whole tomatoes and green chilies, crushed

2 cans (one 15 oz. and one 8 oz.) tomato sauce

1 can (15 oz.) chicken broth

⅛ teaspoon salt

⅛ teaspoon pepper

2 cans (15 oz. each) black beans, liquid included

1 cup baby corn

⅓ cup sliced ripe olives

2 teaspoons minced cilantro leaves

½ cup grated cheddar cheese

In Dutch oven or large heavy saucepan, place 3 tablespoons of the olive oil and heat over medium-high heat. Add chicken and cook, stirring, about 8 minutes or until no longer pink. Remove chicken and wipe pan; add remaining oil, onion, garlic, bell pepper and cumin seed. Stir-fry about 5 minutes; stir in chili powder, oregano, tomatoes and chilies, tomato sauce, chicken broth, salt and pepper. Return chicken to pan, cover, reduce heat to low and simmer about 20 minutes. Add beans, corn and olives. Simmer 15 minutes longer and stir in cilantro. Spoon into serving bowls and sprinkle with cheddar cheese. Makes 6 servings.

Nonfried 'Fried' Chicken Breasts

4 boneless, skinless chicken breast halves

1 cup bread crumbs

2 large cloves garlic, minced

1 tablespoon minced flat-leaf parsley

1 tablespoon minced fresh tarragon

1 teaspoon salt

½ teaspoon freshly ground pepper

1 large egg

3 tablespoons Dijon mustard

¾ cup flour

3 tablespoons olive oil

4 fresh tarragon sprigs

Between two pieces plastic wrap, place chicken and pound gently to even thickness. Line baking sheet with wax paper. In shallow dish, mix together bread crumbs, garlic, parsley, tarragon, salt and pepper. In another dish, beat egg with mustard. Place flour in third dish. Dredge each chicken breast in flour; dip in egg and then bread crumb mixture, covering completely and patting so crumbs adhere. Place on baking sheet (can be prepared ahead), cover with plastic wrap and refrigerate several hours or overnight. Place oil in large nonstick oven-proof frypan; heat over medium-high heat. Add chicken and brown well on both sides. Remove to 350°F. oven and bake just until chicken is cooked through, about 7 minutes, turning once. Transfer to serving plates; garnish each with tarragon sprig. Makes 4 servings.

Chicken Primer

There are basic methods of cooking chicken which are easy to master. Then creativity can take over. Here are things which every cook should know about chicken, its preparation and how to get in on the fun of the next National Chicken Cooking Contest.

Basic Chicken Cookery

Chicken is the most versatile of all meats. It can be prepared in literally hundreds of different ways. However, there are basic cooking methods which everyone should know.

Chicken can be served cooked in any of the following ways. Or, it can be the basis of numerous creative dishes. One 3½ pound chicken usually makes 4 servings. It yields 2½ to 3 cups of cooked, diced chicken.

ROAST CHICKEN. Mix together 1 teaspoon salt and ¼ teaspoon pepper; sprinkle over whole chicken and inside cavity. Hook wing tips under back and place chicken in shallow pan, breast side up. Roast in 350°F. oven about 1 hour or until internal temperature of 180°F. is reached. Let stand 10 minutes before slicing.

FRIED CHICKEN. In plastic bag, mix together ½ cup flour, 1 teaspoon salt and ¼ teaspoon pepper. Add cut-up chicken, a few pieces at a time; shake to coat. In large frypan, place ⅓ cup oil and heat to high temperature. Add chicken, skin side down; cook uncovered about 10 minutes, turning to brown all sides. Reduce heat to medium-low, cover and cook about 20 minutes more or until fork can be inserted with ease. Drain on paper towels.

OVEN-FRIED CHICKEN. In small frypan, melt ¼ cup margarine over medium heat. Remove from heat and stir in 1 teaspoon salt and ¼ teaspoon pepper. In shallow dish, place ½ cup bread crumbs. Using 1 cut-up chicken, dip each part in margarine, then in bread crumbs, turning to coat. On lightly greased baking sheet, arrange chicken, skin side up, in single layer. Bake in 375°F. oven about 50 minutes or until brown and fork tender.

SIMMERED CHICKEN. In deep saucepan, place 1 whole or cut-up chicken. Add 2 cups water, 1 teaspoon salt and ¼ teaspoon pepper (1 small onion sliced and 3 celery tops may also be added, if desired). Cover and simmer about 45 minutes or until fork tender. Remove chicken from pan and cool; reserve broth for later use. Separate meat from bones; discard skin and bones. Dice chicken as desired.

GRILLED CHICKEN. On prepared grill with rack about 8 inches from heat, place chicken halves, quarters or parts. Grill, turning frequently (using tongs to prevent piercing skin), about 1 hour or until tender. Homemade or bottled barbecue sauce may be brushed on chicken during last 15 minutes of grilling time.

MICROWAVE CHICKEN. In shallow microwave dish, arrange chicken with meatier parts toward outside of dish. Brush with browning sauce, if desired, or remove skin and brush with 1 tablespoon melted butter or margarine. Cover with wax paper and microwave on HIGH 18-20 minutes (about 6 minutes per pound), rotating dish ½ turn after 9 minutes. Sprinkle with ½ teaspoon seasoned salt and let stand, covered, 5 minutes. (Note: when microwaving whole bird, set on MEDIUM.)

Test for Doneness

Whatever method is used for cooking chicken, the most accurate test for doneness is a meat thermometer. Whole chicken should reach an internal temperature of 180°F. Bone-in parts should reach a temperature of 170°F. and boneless parts, 160°F. Juices should be clear, not pink, when chicken is pierced with a fork. Normally, chicken is done when a fork can be inserted with ease. Or, when cooking a whole bird, the leg should move freely when lifted or twisted. In microwaving, it is better to undercook than to overcook. Return chicken to microwave for 1 or 2 additional minutes if needed after checking for doneness.

Thawing Chicken

Thaw chicken in refrigerator or in cold water, not on countertop. It takes about 24 hours to thaw a 4 pound chicken in the refrigerator; cut-up parts, 3 to 9 hours.

Chicken Nutrition Chart

	Calories (kcal)	Protein (g)	Total Fat (g)	Saturated Fat (g)
Breast	116	24	2	0
Drumstick	131	23	4	1
Thigh	152	21	7	2
Whole	134	23	4	1
Wing	147	23	6	2

Serving Size: 3 oz. boneless, cooked, skinless portion roasted, braised, broiled/grilled, microwaved, stir-fried or cooked in liquid—without additional fat, salt, sodium or sauces.

Source: USDA data

Meat Comparisons

	Calories (kcal)	Protein (g)	Total Fat (g)	Saturated Fat (g)
Chicken Breast Roasted	165	31	4	1
Beef Tenderloin (lean & fat) Broiled	291	25	20	8
Pork chop, Loin (lean & fat) Broiled	320	22	25	9

Serving Size: 3.5 ounces, cooked

Source: USDA data

Enter

43RD NATIONAL CHICKEN COOKING CONTEST

You could win

$25,000 first prize

$5,000 second	$3,000 third
$2,000 fourth	$1,000 fifth

Finalists will win an

expense-paid trip to the

43rd National Cook-Off

in Dallas, Texas

in 1999

DEADLINE FOR ENTRIES:
October 15, 1998
(see next page for details)

NATIONAL CHICKEN COOKING CONTEST
sponsored by
National Broiler Council
U.S. Poultry & Egg Association

It's Easy to Enter

* Send recipe using broiler-fryer chicken, whole or any part or parts.
* Recipe should be for 4 to 8 servings.
* Recipe must be prepared twice within 3 hour time period.
* Grilling recipes not allowed.
* Entry blank not required. If not available, write name, address and phone number on first page of each recipe.
* Enter as many recipes as you like but each must be on a separate sheet of paper.

RULES

1. Directors and employees of National Broiler Council and U. S. Poultry & Egg Association and their immediate families are not eligible, nor are previous first place winners.

2. Judging will be based on: (1) taste, (2) appearance, (3) simplicity and (4) appeal.

3. Finalists will be selected by an independent recipe judging agency, NOT by random drawing. Each finalist will receive an expense-paid trip to the National Cook-Off in Dallas, TX. Failure to participate in National Cook-Off will result in forfeiture of prize.

4. All entries become property of National Chicken Cooking Contest. Entry constitutes permission to edit, modify, adapt, publish and otherwise use the recipe in any way without compensation.

5. Entries will not be acknowledged or returned. Taxes on prizes are the responsibility of winners. Judges' decisions are final.

6. Any entrant selected for the National Cook-Off who has not reached the age of eighteen by the first day of the Cook-Off proceedings must be accompanied to the Cook-Off by a parent or adult guardian at the entrant's expense.

7. Entries must be original. "Original" is defined as not previously published in the same or substantially the same form. Contestant finalists will be required to certify that the recipe entry is "original."

8. All Contest rules are subject to change by the National Broiler Council and U.S. Poultry & Egg Association without notice.

REMEMBER THE DEADLINE: October 15, 1998.

On each recipe, write name, complete mailing address and telephone number. Mail to:

Chicken Contest
Box 28158 Central Station
Washington, DC 20038-8158

Next Cook-Off Marks
Half Century of Chicken Recipes

Through the years, thousands of recipes have been entered in the National Chicken Cooking Contest, providing a true picture of how America has cooked chicken for the past half century.

The Contest, first held in 1949, has become one of America's leading food competitions. It was an annual event until 1983 when an alternate-year schedule was adopted. Over a half million dollars in prizes have been awarded to cooks across the nation for chicken recipes submitted in the competition.

No one region of the country has a monopoly on good chicken cooks. Cook-Off winners have come from California and Oregon on the West Coast to Connecticut and North Carolina on the East with Michigan and Kansas and other states in between. Winning recipes ranged from dipper's nuggets to chicken pizza to casseroles and imaginative entrées.

It's easy to get in on the fun and perhaps win an expense-paid trip to Dallas, Texas, to take part in the 43rd National Cook-Off in Spring, 1999. National Cook-Off finalists will compete there for the top prize of $25,000. Four others will divide an additional $11,000 in prize money.

Just write name, address and telephone number on the front of a favorite chicken recipe(s) and mail before the October 15, 1998, deadline. (See complete details for entering on page 120.)

Recipes in the first part of this book are the 51 finalists from which judges had the difficult task of selecting the five best prepared in the 42nd National Chicken Cooking Contest held in Hilton Head, South Carolina. Winners from previous Cook-Offs are also included in the book, along with recipes from some of the nation's leading chefs and other enticing ways to prepare chicken.

Try them and then start developing your own recipes. Chicken is so versatile you'll never run out of ideas for serving America's favorite meat.

Past Chicken Cooking Champions

1971	Norma Young, Arkansas	Dipper's Nuggets Chicken
1972	Carol Pfeiffer, Delaware	Chicken Pot-au-Feu
1973	Clement Holley, Delaware	Chicken Asparagus Casserole
1974	Fayne Lutz, New Mexico	Hot Chinese Chicken Salad
1975	Caroline Graefe, Idaho	Chicken 'n Swiss Extraordinaire
1976	Thomas Parvis, New Jersey	Sunshine Chicken
1977	Ann Costa, Georgia	Chicken Ratatouille
1978	Mary Cerami, California	Chicken Pizza
1979	Barbara Long, Wyoming	Curried Chicken Rolls
1980	Sheila Hoban, District of Columbia	Capital Chicken Casserole
1981	June Herke, South Dakota	Impossible Chicken Pie
1982	Marcia Adams, Indiana	Baked Chicken Reuben
1983	Karen Johnson, Kansas	Chicken with Lime Butter
1985	Sally Vog, Oregon	Chicken Picante
1987	Marjorie Fortier, Connecticut	Chicken Avocado Melt
1989	Melissa Mathie, Michigan	Summer Italian Stuffed Chicken
1991	Judith Markiewicz, Ohio	Southwestern Oven-Fried Chicken
1993	Rosemarie Berger, North Carolina	Caribbean Chicken Drums
1995	Mary Louise Lever, Georgia	Baked Spicy Pineapple Balinese Chicken

The Chicken Cookbook

Additional copies of *The Chicken Cookbook* are available at the special price of $2.00 each only from the National Broiler Council.

To order, send a check or money order (no cash) to:

Chicken Cookbook
Department NBC
Box 307
Coventry, Connecticut 06238

Be sure to include your name and complete mailing address, the number of copies desired and a check or money order to cover the cost @$2.00 each.

The Chicken Cookbook is also sold at select outlets across the country at the regular price of $4.99.

Index